THE MODERN KEBAB

60 recipes from

EBURY
PRESS

Contents

Introduction

Friends Stephen Tozer and Ed Brunet loved kebabs. They loved the simple gastronomic concept of charcoal-grilled meats with soft, chewy flatbreads and piquant salads. They were inspired by the rustically delicious kebabs they had eaten abroad, but they wanted more than they had found back home.

Kebabs, like most ancient dishes, are a product of terroir. Their traditional form was dictated by the best, most beautiful, naturally occurring ingredients. Wild and extensively farmed animals provided the meat. Garnishes came from seasonal or preserved vegetables, fruits and herbs – plants cultivated without chemicals and outside artificial environments. Open fires that were fuelled by wood from the same land, and necessary for human subsistence, were used to cook them.

And this is the way that all food should be. When food emanates from good and natural ingredients, it tastes best. Fruits and vegetables taste best when they are at their freshest, and have been grown without coercion. Preserves taste best when they are made from the best fruits and vegetables. Meat is at its best when it comes from animals that have grown at a steady pace, on a proper diet, in expansive conditions. Beyond ingredients, fire-cooking has a special primal significance to us. As the earliest means of heating food, fire has been present through the entire history of cookery. Smell (as opposed to taste, or texture) is the one constituent of flavour with the ability to trigger memories in the brain. While the high heat of fire-grilling produces caramelised, umami-heavy flavour via the Maillard reaction, fire cooking's unique contribution to food is aromatisation. The 'flavour' conferred only by fire is experienced predominantly via our sense of smell. Consequently, it taps into our evolutionary food instincts in a unique way.

In kebabs, Stephen and Ed also saw an opportunity to use modern techniques and approaches to elevate a dish uniformly coloured by tradition. While tradition in food holds huge value, if observed too rigorously it can also represent a constraint. Fresh ideas and techniques at the forefront of gastronomic thinking are continuously unlocking new and improved ways of enjoying our food. A sympathetic application of modern cookery can elevate even the greatest traditional dishes.

Stephen and Ed wanted to eat kebabs that obeyed these principles. They wanted modern, fire-cooked kebabs. They wanted kebabs that delivered maximally intense flavour by honouring the terroir of where they were served, and using excellent local meat. Kebabs like this did not exist. So they founded Le Bab. Joined by Manu Canales and Angus Bell, they began to experiment with a new kind of kebab. In January 2016 they opened their first restaurant in Soho, London.

Le Bab is simply about trying to make kebabs as good as they can be. At the epicentre of the project is a resolute belief in the primacy of ingredients in good food, and in the primacy of terroir in good ingredients. We seek to lovingly turn these ingredients into kebabs using the best possible ideas and techniques; we want to cook them, marry them and mingle them with maximum skill and imagination. We can distil this into three interlinked core tenets: ingredients, concept and technique.

INGREDIENTS

The UK is not a motherland of the kebab. Its cool winters and tepid, often rainy summers mean it is not a natural home to the ingredients of traditional kebabs. Only hardier plants can survive the winter frosts. The fruits and vegetables of the eastern Mediterranean and Middle East struggle to thrive outside the height of summer, if at all.

However, the UK is a producer of phenomenal meat, fish, vegetables and fruit. We seek to utilise these ingredients when they are at their best. Our proteins, vegetables and fruits form the major 'backbone' of taste in our dishes, and so their quality is always of the utmost importance.

Pastoral farming practices in the UK lead the world. We have a wealth of meat produced by farmers that resolutely pursue optimal flavour, through meticulous breeding and rearing. The British countryside is home to exceptional and diverse wild game. And our butchers are masters of hanging and dry-ageing.

Britain's seafood is also world class. British waters are cold and clean. Their temperatures mean a good concentration of oxygen, lower solubility of toxins, and a lower growth of pathogenic microbes than in warmer waters. Fish and shellfish benefit from the cool, strong currents of the Atlantic coast, growing slowly and proliferating higher amounts of omega-3 fatty acids. We also have a strong culture of sustainable fishing, with a large number of day boats providing supremely fresh catches.

While the UK could not claim to be a world leader in arable produce, we do produce exceptional brassica and root vegetables. Our wet summers also mean lighter produce that might traditionally be associated with kebabs – tomatoes and lettuce are produced to an excellent standard for a few months each year.

We feel compelled to utilise these excellent ingredients. We eschew the approach of importing ingredients from abroad to avoid a seasonal dearth of certain ingredients. In doing so we celebrate and encourage excellent farming practices, and minimise environmental impact.

We urge you to go out and shop seasonally, trying to construct your food from produce grown and reared naturally and as close to home as possible.

CONCEPT

We work backwards from the best ingredients available to us to the concept of each dish we serve. This provides a framework for concept and design. We also seek to deliver food that excites and surprises people, and obeys certain gastronomic principles to deliver the best eating experience and make people feel like they are consuming an authentic kebab.

As talked about, ingredients are at the heart of our food philosophy. In allying ourselves to regional and seasonal produce, we must find ways to deliver spices and flavours from the eastern kebab heartlands, whilst staying true to the brilliant macro ingredients that deliver the best and most intense core tastes.

This is all about finding flavour combinations that both work and evoke a strong sense of 'kebab', despite often being unorthodox. A dish must ultimately represent a harmony of its component parts: typically a carbohydrate, a protein, several vegetables and herbs, with spicing and sauces to unify and enhance the dish. It must also have the spice, the intensity and the piquancy of a traditional kebab. We continuously think about and experiment with what works, and what might work, in each respect.

In doing what we do, we often emerge with recipes that challenge preconceptions about what a kebab 'should' be or contain. Our kebabs contain meats and garnishes that are unfamiliar in orthodox kebabs, but have been rigorously and carefully constructed. We hope that this surprises and delights those who eat them.

TECHNIQUE

Our founding kitchen team comprises three chefs with extensive Michelin experience, predominantly in classic and modern European kitchens. This brings a totally different technical approach to our cookery. We are able to deploy methods and techniques that have been honed in the Michelin world, at the cutting edge of gastronomy. These are methods designed to extract maximal flavour from ingredients, and to perfect their textures. We try to apply techniques subtly and sparingly, so as only to enhance our kebabs without damaging their simplicity.

Given our belief in the primacy of ingredients, we cherish technique as a way of ensuring that no ingredient is mistreated. Concurrently, to over-apply cooking techniques or to over-process the produce that we work with would be to go against our principles. Instead, we seek to cook only as much as we have to, and in ways that are minimally invasive to the essence of our produce. Technique enables us to celebrate ingredients, and to ensure they are never wasted nor devalued.

A purée can sometimes be a brilliant way of enhancing a certain ingredient's flavour, and enveloping a dish in it. A pickle or souse can help to soften or tame a strong natural taste, while retaining its essence and providing acidity that lifts a whole dish. Frying and roasting can intensify flavours whilst bringing crispy or crunchy texture. Sometimes, leaving something totally raw can be exactly the right thing to do. The essence of our cookery is gentle manipulation of select ingredients to bring contrast and harmony to our food, whilst retaining their essence through delicacy of touch. No ingredient should be used, or processed, in vain.

Le Bab Cooking Techniques

- We recommend cooking all your meats and fish on a barbecue. However, as this is not always possible, we will also show you how you can cook the kebabs using a frying or chargrill pan or under the grill.

- Ahead of the cooking time, take your meat and fish out of the fridge to come to room temperature.

- We recommend to prep all your meat and fish at home, for fun and the learning experience. However, if your space or time is limited, you can always ask the butcher or fishmonger to do it for you – they will usually do a great job.

- It is difficult for us to tell you how hot your barbecue should be. It depends on many factors and you cannot regulate it like an oven or hob, so cooking times may vary if you are using the barbecue.

- When you are ready to cook, unless something different is specified in the recipe, start by applying a gentle heat to the ingredients.

- Many of our recipes involve skewering ingredients to cook over a barbecue. It makes a huge difference if you're able to invest in some proper skewers, available at many good Middle Eastern grocery or general stores. These are typically flat and broad (1–2 cm) with a pointed, triangular tip, as opposed to the thin, circular items usually sold in this country.

Proper skewers will hold the pieces threaded onto them securely rather than the pieces slipping around as the skewers are turned. They will distribute heat better to the centre of the ingredients for optimal cooking.

- Always take into consideration the residual heat, meaning that your meat or fish will continue cooking while it is off the heat and resting, though this will be at a slower pace and not for long. We recommend to take the meat or fish off the heat before it has come to the desired point of cooking, and let it get there off the heat. When to do it depends mostly on the size of the cut and how the cooking has been. We have tried to specify where we can but, like everything, you will master this by practice.

- We pride ourselves on making everything in the restaurant, including all our sauces, breads and pickles. However, we understand that home cooking is different and people might not have the time or space for storage. So, though we encourage you to have a go at making everything yourself and have included in the book basic recipes that we use in many of our dishes (see page 110), we can also suggest that you try some of the great products you can find in many shops now, including tomato sauce, harissa paste, chilli sauce, mayo, za'atar and so on.

Mezze

Le babaganoush

Our version of the classic smoked aubergine purée.

4 aubergines
Extra virgin olive oil
Handful of coriander

1. Place the whole aubergines on top of some tin foil, season, add a drizzle of olive oil and wrap them up in the foil. Cook in the oven at 160°C/315°F/Gas mark 2 for about 35 minutes until you can run a toothpick through one without resistance.

2. Let the aubergines cool down and then take the skin off and discard. Place the flesh into a bowl and whisk vigorously with a hand whisk while you add about 3 tablespoons olive oil to emulsify it and create a creamy consistency. Season and sprinkle with a handful of chopped coriander, and serve as a dip.

Cauliflower pastilla

Meat-lovers adore this vegetarian dish. Intense, spicy cauliflower encased in a fine, crisp pastry, with a sweet, creamy and slightly acidic pineapple yoghurt to lift it. Buy brick pastry in Arabic supermarkets, or try using puff pastry instead.

FOR THE PASTILLA

200 g cauliflower, broken into florets

25 g unsalted butter

1 teaspoon cayenne pepper

1 teaspoon ground turmeric

1 teaspoon garam masala

1 teaspoon ground cumin

1 teaspoon ground coriander

100 g plain flour

6 sheets brick pastry

Vegetable oil, for frying

FOR THE YOGHURT DIP

200 g full-fat Greek yoghurt

½ pineapple, diced into 1 cm squares

1 handful of fresh coriander, roughly chopped

1. Blitz the raw cauliflower florets in a food processor until they are the texture of couscous, discarding the cauliflower's tough internal stem. Melt the butter in a pan and let it bubble away for a minute or so until it just begins to turn brown. Add the cauliflower 'couscous', turn down the heat to very low and let it cook slowly for an hour, stirring often, until it is soft and slightly golden.

2. Take the pan from the heat, add the spices and a pinch of salt and stir through whilst the cauliflower is still hot. Let it cool before dividing the mixture into six equal-sized sausages, about 10 cm long.

3. To roll the pastilla, mix the plain flour in a bowl with about 75 ml water to make a paste. Lay a sheet of the brick pastry down on a clean surface and put one of the cauliflower sausage shapes on the bottom curve of the pastry, about 2.5 cm from the edge. Roll the pastry over the top of the pastilla mix, before folding the left and right sides of the pastry sheet inwards, using the paste to stick them down and making sure there are no air bubbles trapped inside. Then, roll the pastilla from the bottom of the sheet to the top, again making sure it is rolled tightly, and using a little more of the paste at the top of the sheet of pastry to secure. The pastilla will look like a spring roll. Repeat with the remaining pastry sheets and filling.

4. Mix together all the ingredients for the yoghurt dip.

5. To cook the pastilla, deep or shallow fry them at 180°C in a flavourless vegetable oil until they are golden and crisp. Season the outside, cut in half with a small serrated knife and serve alongside the yoghurt dip.

Endive and pomegranate salad

A simple salad showcasing a beautiful winter leaf. Jewels of pomegranate contrast with the sour sumac and bitter endive, with shallots adding a savoury allium kick.

FOR THE SALAD

4 white endive

4 red endive

Seeds of 1 pomegranate

1 shallot, finely sliced into rings

Sumac

FOR THE DRESSING

2 tablespoons white wine vinegar

2 tablespoons extra virgin olive oil

1. Slice off the very end of the endive to separate their leaves, give them a good wash and let them drain. Mix these leaves with the pomegranate seeds and shallot rings before sprinkling with sumac and a little salt.

2. Just before serving, dress the leaves with the white wine vinegar and olive oil and arrange in a bowl, making sure you can see the pomegranate seeds and shallot rings.

Devilled eggs

A devilled filling of sulphurous egg-yolk and smoky babaganoush is enriched by mayonnaise in this harmony of vegetarian flavours. The better the egg, the better this will be.

2 aubergines

Extra virgin olive oil

6 eggs

½ teaspoon cayenne pepper

1 teaspoon smoked paprika

1 teaspoon ground cumin

50 g Le Bab Mayonnaise
  (see page 116)

TO SERVE

Finely chopped fresh chives

1. Place the whole aubergines on top of some tin foil, season, add a drizzle of olive oil and wrap them up in the foil. Cook in the oven at 160°C/315°F/Gas mark 2 for about 35 minutes until you can run a toothpick through one without resistance.

2. Let the aubergines cool down and then take the skin off and discard. Place the flesh into a bowl and season.

3. Boil the eggs for 12 minutes, then straight away add to iced water, peel and halve them. Take the yolks out carefully so as not to break the egg white halves and mix the yolks with the aubergine, spices and mayo. Season and give the mixture a good stir until evenly combined. Scoop over the egg white halves. Sprinkle the top with some finely chopped chives.

Levantine haggis

Our take on a nose-to-tail Scottish classic, combining lamb offal with Levantine herbs and spices. The piquancy of the Levantine ingredients helps to cut across and lift the offal flavour. Buy the goat's pluck and lamb fat from your butcher.

1 goat's pluck, trimmed
500 g rolled oats
3 onions, finely diced
5 garlic cloves, finely chopped
25 g fresh coriander, chopped
25 g fresh parsley, chopped
1 tablespoon cayenne pepper
20 g ground cumin
15 g ground coriander
2 teaspoons grated nutmeg
2 teaspoons ground cinnamon
50 g salt
400 g lamb channel fat, grated
4 eggs
4 slices of bread

1. Thoroughly wash the goat's pluck to remove any blood clots, then trim and discard any connective tissue to leave just the heart, lungs and liver. Put these through a mincer. If you do not have a mincer at home, or are not confident at dealing with offal, ask your butcher to do this for you.

2. Preheat the oven to 170°C/325°F/Gas mark 3. Toast the oats on a baking tray for about 45 minutes, giving them a shake every 10 minutes, until they are golden brown.

3. Mix the onion, garlic, fresh herbs, spices, salt, lamb fat and oats through the minced pluck. Shape into patties roughly the size of burgers before frying with a little oil in a non-stick frying pan for 5 minutes until cooked through.

4. Fry the eggs and toast the bread, then serve the haggis patties on a piece of toast, topped with a fried egg.

Mutton meatballs

A simple meatball with the powerful flavour of mutton, served in a rich and sweet tomato sauce with Arabic spices.

800 g lamb mince
Olive oil
40 g pitted dates
600 g vine tomatoes
50 g pomegranate molasses

FOR THE LAMB SPICE

2 teaspoons ground cumin
1 teaspoon biber or red chilli pepper paste
1 teaspoon sumac
1 small onion, finely diced
1 garlic clove, finely grated
2 tablespoons chopped fresh parsley leaves
2 tablespoons fresh thyme leaves
2 teaspoons soy sauce

TO SERVE

40g roasted peanuts, crushed
1 small handful of picked coriander leaves

1. Spice the lamb mince by mixing through the cumin, biber, sumac, onion, garlic, parsley, thyme and soy sauce thoroughly.

2. Drizzle some oil in a pan and cook the spiced lamb over a medium–high heat to help with the colouring.

3. Blitz together the dates and the tomatoes in a food processor and add to the lamb. Let everything cook and reduce until it gets to the consistency of a Bolognese sauce. Add the molasses and keep cooking until it becomes a sticky consistency. Season well.

4. Place a large saucepan over a high heat with a little olive oil. Add the meatballs and cook them until well caramelised all over, approximately 2–3 minutes. If your pan is not big enough, it is better to do this in a couple of batches so as not to overcrowd it. Return all the meatballs to the pan and add the sauce. Turn down the heat and simmer for 20 minutes until the meatballs are cooked through.

5. To serve, place a few meatballs in each dish, spoon over a generous amount of sauce and top with some roasted peanuts and coriander.

Grilled cheese

A great way to use up spare flatbreads the day after they are made. This is like a Mexican quesadilla, using our staple charred chilli sauce. Use a good aged Cheddar for ultimate flavour.

1 portion of Le Bab Chilli Sauce
(see page 117)

4 Le Bab Flatbreads (see page 112)
80 g Cheddar cheese, grated

1. On one flatbread, and depending on how you like heat, spread a good amount of the chilli sauce before sprinkling half the grated cheese on top. Top with a second flatbread. Repeat with the other two flatbreads.

2. In a non-stick frying pan large enough to fit your flatbreads, fry each flatbread sandwich over medium heat for 5–6 minutes, turning halfway, until the cheese is melted and the flatbreads are crispy. Cut into slices and serve.

Bobby bean salad

This deliciously zippy salad is a brilliant summer dish. It contrasts the intense, fragrant acidity of the lime with the sweetness and richness of roasted almonds and the delicate flavour of the best summer beans.

600 g bobby or green beans

2 kohlrabi

FOR THE TOASTED CHILLI ALMONDS

100 g whole blanched almonds

4 teaspoons carob syrup

Couple of pinches of chilli flakes

FOR THE DRESSING

2 teaspoons fresh lime juice

4 teaspoons carob syrup

1 tablespoon olive oil

TO SERVE

1 large handful of fresh chervil

1. Bring a pan of seasoned water to the boil. Top and tail the beans, then throw them into the boiling water for a minute or two – they should still have a crunch. Drain and put them into salted ice water. Peel the kohlrabi, dice into 2 cm chunks and set aside for later.

2. Toast the almonds in the oven at 170°C/325°F/Gas mark 3 for 10 minutes until a little golden. Remove from the oven and toss in the carob syrup and chilli flakes, then return to the oven for a couple of minutes.

3. Squeeze the lime juice into a jug and add the carob syrup and olive oil. Whisk to combine and add a pinch of salt.

4. Season the vegetables and toss with the dressing. Top the salad with the almonds and chervil leaves to serve.

Meatlafel

One of our favourite dishes: an indulgent take on the classic falafel, with unctuous braised meat encased in crisp herby falafel.

FOR THE FALAFEL MIX

250 g dried chickpeas
500 g frozen peas
1 onion, roughly chopped
2 garlic cloves
20 g fresh parsley
20 g fresh coriander
1 teaspoon ground cumin
1 teaspoon ground coriander
10 g gram flour
Oil, for frying

FOR THE MEAT STUFFING

300 g lamb shoulder, diced
300 g beef shin, sliced by your butcher
  so it is still with the bone
4 litres water
80 g tomato paste
1 teaspoon cayenne pepper
2 teaspoons ground cumin
2 teaspoons smoked paprika

TO SERVE

1 portion of Tzatziki (see page 41)

1. Soak the dried chickpeas overnight in plenty of water. The next morning, drain them and blitz in a food processor to a coarse paste.

2. Dehydrate the frozen peas at 140°C/275°F/Gas mark 1 for about 20 minutes, until wrinkled yet not totally dry. Allow them to cool before also blitzing them in a food processor.

3. Blitz the remaining falafel ingredients into a paste and combine with the blitzed chickpeas and peas. Season with salt. At this point it is a good idea to deep or shallow fry a small portion of falafel at around 160°C, just to make sure the mixture holds. If it falls apart in the fryer, it may be too wet, so add a little more gram flour and try again.

4. In a pot, colour the meat, then add 4 litres water. Simmer for around 2½ hours until the meat is completely soft and falls off the bone. If towards the end of the cooking time all the water has evaporated, keep adding water. If not, keep reducing until it becomes like a thick paste. Add the tomato paste and spices, season and cook gently for 10 minutes. Chill or just leave to cool.

5. Once cool, roll the meat into 20 g balls with your hands and place on a clean plate. Roll the falafel mix into 25 g balls. On the palm of your hand, flatten a falafel ball before placing a stuffing ball on it and topping it with another flattened falafel ball. Seal with your fingertips until the meat is thoroughly covered. Repeat with the remaining balls.

6. When you are ready to serve, fry the meatlafel balls at 160°C in a little oil in a deep-fat fryer or in a deep-sided frying pan until they are brown and crispy. Remove from the fryer onto some paper towels, season with salt and serve with a dollop of Tzatziki.

Heritage tomato salad

A seasonal extravaganza: British heritage tomatoes with a simple dressing that lets their phenomenal natural flavour shine through.

600 g varied heritage tomatoes

2 tablespoons white balsamic vinegar

2 tablespoons extra virgin olive oil

Za'atar

1. Cut the tomatoes into chunks and slices, making sure you have a varied selection of colours and types. Just before serving, season and dress with the balsamic vinegar, olive oil and a few strands of the za'atar.

Duck ragú

An intensely spiced ragú of duck leg, which is braised slowly to yield soft and tender meat. Rich, delicious and moreish.

FOR THE RAGÚ

4 duck legs

Vegetable oil

1 onion, diced

1 garlic clove, grated

1 teaspoon chilli flakes

1 teaspoon ground turmeric

1 whole star anise

4 green cardamom pods

1 teaspoon ground cinnamon

1 teaspoon grated nutmeg

1 teaspoon ground cloves

1 kg large vine tomatoes

FOR THE DATE SCONES

200 g self-raising flour

1 teaspoon baking powder

A pinch of salt

20 g caster sugar

60 g unsalted butter, at room temperature

50 g pitted dates, diced to the size of raisins

100 ml whole milk

1 egg, beaten

1. In a deep pan, brown the skin of the duck legs in some vegetable oil on both sides, then set aside. In the same pan, fry the onion until soft before adding the garlic and spices. Season and fry for a couple of minutes over a low heat to release the flavours. In a food processor, blitz the tomatoes until smooth before adding them, along with about 1 litre of water and the duck legs, and cook for about 2 hours until the meat is falling off the legs.

2. Remove the legs from the sauce and strip them of the flesh, discarding the bones and skin. Meanwhile, reduce the tomato sauce down until thick and any excess water has evaporated, before removing the cardamom pods and star anise and returning the picked duck flesh to the pan. Season.

3. To make the date scones, mix together the dry ingredients. Cube the butter and rub it into the flour mixture with your fingertips until you have a sandy texture. Add the dates. Make a well in the centre and pour in the milk. Mix it together, being careful not to overwork the flour. Once the dough is mixed, divide it into six equal-sized portions and roll these into balls. Brush with the beaten egg before cooking at 180°C/350°F/Gas mark 4 for 20 minutes.

4. Halve the scones and serve the duck ragú on top.

Green salad with pea and mint

Summer on a plate. Crisp lettuce, sweet peas, with light, delicate mint and a bitter-sweet-sour dressing to complement.

FOR THE DRESSING

150 g peas, cooked
1 handful of fresh mint leaves
140 ml extra virgin olive oil
45 ml white wine vinegar

FOR THE SALAD

½ cucumber
4 baby gem lettuces, leaves separated
Pea shoots

1. Blitz together the peas with the mint, oil and vinegar in a food processor until it comes together. Season.

2. Cut the cucumber in half lengthways and scrape out the seeds. Dice it into cubes. Dress the lettuce and cucumber with the pea dressing and top the salad with the pea shoots.

Hummus

Using a variety of alternative pulses gives this hummus an unusual flavour, higher in umami than traditional versions. The spicing gives a complex, fragrant undertone. The garlic can be tweaked to your liking.

90 g dried chickpeas
40 g dried borlotti beans
20 g dried puy lentils
½ whole star anise
½ whole black cardamom pod
1 garlic clove
50 ml olive oil
A squeeze of lemon juice (optional)

TO SERVE
Baby radishes

1. The night before you want to make the hummus, soak the chickpeas and borlotti beans in plenty of cold water for at least 12 hours.

2. The next day, drain the soaked beans and place them in a pan along with the puy lentils, star anise, black cardamom pod, plenty of salt and more than enough water to cover. Bring to a gentle boil and cook the beans and lentils for about 1½ hours until totally soft, adding more water if necessary.

3. Drain, remove the star anise and black cardamom pod and allow the beans to cool slightly before blending in a food processor with the garlic clove, 180 ml water and the oil. If the hummus gets too thick, add a little more water. Season to taste, and add a little lemon juice if you like a zesty flavour. Serve with baby radishes for a sweet crunch.

Merguez and chickpea ragú

A comforting ragú made using chickpeas and traditional North African lamb (or mutton) sausages.

5 Merguez sausages
250 g chickpeas (in brine)
150 g Swiss chard or spinach leaves
250 ml chicken stock
100 g salted butter

1. Dice the sausages and start frying them in a deep pan.

2. Meanwhile, drain the chickpeas and rinse them under running water. Cut the chard or spinach leaves to bite-sized pieces. Once the sausages are coloured all around, add the stock to the pan and let it reduce until it thickens but isn't on the verge of totally evapourating. Add the chickpeas and the butter, give a nice stir and finally, off the heat, add the leaves and keep stirring – they will wilt with the residual heat. Season and serve.

Grilled sardines

Serves 4

Grilled sardines with a simple, zesty garnish are a trans-Mediterranean classic. This dish is all about top-quality fish treated simply, so find the best sardines you can.

4 slices of sourdough bread
Extra virgin olive oil
8 fresh sardines, filleted
Le Bab chilli sauce (see page 117)
Zest of 1 lemon

1. Season the slices of bread with salt and a little oil and place the bread on a baking tray. Toast them at around 160°C/315°F/Gas mark 2, turning every 5 minutes or so, until crisp. Remove from the oven but keep the oven on, turning the temperature up to high.

2. Heat a barbecue or chargrill pan. Season the fish with a little salt and some olive oil and place skin-side down. If the skin sticks, your barbecue or chargrill pan is not hot enough. Cook for around 30 seconds before turning the fish over and cooking the other side for another 30 seconds. Check the fish – if it is still a little raw for your liking, you can flash it in the hot oven if you wish.

3. Spread a little chilli sauce on each of the dried toasts and put the sardine fillets on top. Sprinkle some lemon zest over them.

Lahmacun

Our Lahmacun is a savoury mille-feuille of flatbread and lamb sauce, inspired by the Ottoman classic sometimes referred to as "Turkish pizza".

800 g lamb mince

Olive oil

40 g pitted dates

600 g vine tomatoes

50 g pomegranate molasses

FOR THE LAMB SPICE

2 teaspoons ground cumin

1 teaspoon biber or red chilli pepper paste

1 teaspoon sumac

1 small onion, finely diced

1 garlic clove, finely grated

2 tablespoons chopped fresh parsley leaves

2 tablespoons fresh thyme leaves

2 teaspoons soy sauce

TO SERVE

4 stale Le Bab Flatbreads (see page 112)

1 portion of Tzatziki (see page 41)

1. Spice the lamb mince by mixing through the cumin, biber, sumac, onion, garlic, parsley, thyme and soy sauce thoroughly.

2. Drizzle some oil in a pan and cook the spiced lamb over a medium–high heat to help with the colouring.

3. Blitz together the dates and the tomatoes in a food processor and add to the lamb. Let everything cook and reduce until it gets to the consistency of a Bolognese sauce. Add the molasses and keep cooking until it becomes a sticky consistency. Season and set aside.

4. Build the lahmacun by spreading the meat sauce on a flatbread and building the layers, repeating the process until the sauce and flatbreads are used up – it will look like a round lasagne. Flash it in the oven at 150°C/300°F/Gas mark 2 for a few minutes to heat up, then cut it in triangles like a pizza. Serve with some Tzatziki as a dip.

Scotch kofte

Scotch egg "a la plancha", with a smoky kick. Use a top-quality egg to richly contrast the warmly spiced exterior of minced pork.

500 g pork mince

FOR THE PORK SPICE

20 g smoked paprika

20 g ground cumin

1 small onion, finely diced

6 eggs

FOR THE BROWN SAUCE

500 g vine tomatoes

Olive oil

1 small onion, diced

50 g pitted dates

50 ml white wine vinegar

2 teaspoons smoked paprika

1 tablespoon chilli flakes

1 teaspoon brown sugar

50 g pomegranate molasses

1. To make the brown sauce, blitz the tomatoes in a food processor until smooth and liquid. Heat some olive oil in a pan and fry the onion until soft and golden, before adding all the other ingredients. Simmer gently for an hour or so until the excess water has evaporated and you are left with a thick, dark sauce. Season and remove from the heat. Blend to a smooth purée in the food processor and put into a sterilised kilner jar. You can keep this sauce for up to a week.

2. Whilst you wait for the brown sauce to cook, thoroughly combine the minced pork with the paprika, cumin, diced onion and a good amount of salt. Cook a small ball of the spiced pork to check the seasoning, adding more salt if it tastes a bit bland. Divide the remaining pork into six 80 g balls and put to one side.

3. Boil the eggs in plenty of water for about 4½ minutes (this is the cooking time for eggs at room temperature – if your eggs have been kept in the fridge the cooking time will be longer). You want the egg whites to be firm but the yolks to be runny still. As soon as the eggs come out of the boiling water, you need to drop them into a bowl of icy water to stop them cooking any longer, otherwise your Scotch eggs will not have a runny centre. Once the eggs are thoroughly cooled, peel them and pat them dry.

4. To form the kofte, cover a chopping board with cling film to stop the pork mince from sticking to it, before flattening one ball of the mince to the thickness of about 5 mm. Place a peeled egg in the middle and wrap the mince around it, sealing it with your fingers. Do the same with the five remaining balls of meat and eggs.

5. To cook the kofte, place on an extremely hot chargrill pan or on the barbecue to get a little colour on the outside of the kofte. If the meat sticks, your pan or barbecue is not hot enough. Put into a hot oven at 225°C/425°F/Gas mark 7 for 7 minutes, so that when you cut one open the pork mince is cooked through but the egg is still soft. Serve with a dollop of the brown sauce.

Celeriac and beetroot slaw

A healthy coleslaw alternative that uses raw winter roots. The quality of the vegetables is everything in this dish, and the UK grows some of the best beetroot and celeriac in the world.

1 celeriac

3 red beetroot

80 g Le Bab Mayonnaise
(see page 116)

Alfalfa sprouts

1. Chop the very top and the very bottom off the celeriac, peel and discard the skin. Cut the celeriac into thin slices and then cut again to obtain matchstick shapes. Do the same for the beetroot and keep them separate.

2. Season the matchsticks and dress with mayonnaise, keeping the beetroot and celeriac separate if you don't want to mix the colours. Serve topped with alfalfa sprouts.

Sprouting broccoli and Worcestershire hollandaise

Char-grilling broccoli brings out an incredible umami flavour, accentuated by the addition of Worcestershire sauce in an indulgent hollandaise. As punchy a vegetable dish as any.

50 g whole blanched almonds
500 g purple sprouting broccoli
Olive oil

FOR THE WORCESTERSHIRE HOLLANDAISE

250 g clarified butter
2 egg yolks
2 teaspoons white wine vinegar
50 ml Worcestershire sauce

1. Toast the almonds in the oven at 170°C/325°F/Gas mark 3 for 10 minutes until a little golden. Remove from the oven.

2. Melt the clarified butter in a small pan. Place the egg yolks, 2 teaspoons water and the vinegar in another deep pan. Over a very low heat (or in a gently simmering bain-marie if instead of a pan you are using a bowl) start whisking vigorously, while you slowly add the clarified butter until everything is incorporated. Now, off the heat, add the Worcestershire sauce and if you think it is too thick, add a little water to loosen it up. Season. Cover and keep somewhere warm but not hot.

3. Trim the hard bottoms off the sprouting broccoli so you are left with the tender part. Drizzle some olive oil over them and season. Ideally using a chargrill pan, cook them over a medium heat, turning them every so often until they are coloured and tender but still have a bite to them. Once they are ready, transfer them on to a serving tray or individual plates and pour over some hollandaise and roasted almonds.

Taramasalata

A classic. Taramasalata is an umami-rich paté made from smoked cod's roe.

200 g smoked cod's roe
65 g white bread
45 ml whole milk
15 g Dijon mustard
2 garlic cloves
55 ml vegetable oil

1. The cod's roe will be in a skin that needs to be peeled away. Cut the crusts off the bread, then slice it into smaller rough pieces and soak them in the milk for a few minutes. Place all the ingredients apart from the oil into the blender. Blitz and slowly add the oil. If the taramasalata becomes too thick, then just add a little more water. Once all the oil is added, season and immediately chill before serving.

Tzatziki

Another classic, Tzatziki is brightened by the clean acidity of lemon juice and peppery extra virgin olive oil.

500 g full-fat Greek yoghurt
2 tablespoons extra virgin olive oil
1 tablespoon fresh lemon juice
½ cucumber
2 garlic cloves

1. In a large mixing bowl, tip in the yoghurt, the olive oil and the lemon juice. Cut the cucumber in half and scrape out the seeds with a teaspoon. Discard the seeds and grate the flesh and skin into the bowl. Grate the garlic on the fine side of the grater and then give it one last chop before adding it to the mix as well. Season the Tzatziki to taste. Give it a final mix and serve alongside some bread or with the main course.

Mains

Pork shawarma hash

Fried egg, tater tots and brown sauce

Serves 4

8 thick slices of streaky bacon

FOR THE BROWN SAUCE

1 kg vine tomatoes

1 onion, diced

Olive oil

100 g dates, pitted

100 ml white wine vinegar

4 teaspoons smoked paprika

10 g chilli flakes

10 g brown sugar

100 g pomegranate molasses

FOR THE TATER TOTS

3 baking potatoes

1 onion, finely diced

Plain flour

Oil, for frying

FOR THE BACON SPICE

2 teaspoons cayenne pepper

2 teaspoons ground cinnamon

1 teaspoon ground cloves

1½ teaspoons ground coriander

½ teaspoon ground nutmeg

1 tablespoon freshly ground
black pepper

1 tablespoon ground turmeric

1 teaspoon fennel seeds

15 g ground cumin

TO SERVE

4 eggs

Ultimate brunch comfort food. The brown sauce unifies this dish, working brilliantly with each individual element, so be liberal with it! Use thick cut bacon if you can.

1. To make the brown sauce, first blitz the tomatoes in a food processor until smooth. Fry the onion in a little oil until soft and golden, before adding all the other ingredients. Simmer gently for an hour or so until the excess water has evaporated and you are left with a thick, dark sauce. Season, remove from the heat, blend to a smooth purée and pour into a sterilised kilner jar.

2. To make the tater tots, bake the potatoes at 180°C/350°F/Gas mark 4 for around an hour, until you can poke a skewer through them easily. Allow to cool before scooping out the insides and mixing with the diced onion, some salt and freshly ground black pepper in a bowl. Using your hands, form the potato into cylinders around 5 cm long and 1.5 cm in diameter. Roll the tots in the plain flour and put to one side, ready to fry.

3. Mix the bacon spices together and rub a little on the bacon slices before grilling in the oven or on a barbecue. There is no need to season the meat as bacon is already salty. Whilst the bacon is cooking, fry the four eggs in a non-stick frying pan. Deep or shallow fry the tater tots for about 3–4 minutes until golden brown and crispy, before draining onto some paper towels.

4. On each plate, put a couple of pieces of the spiced bacon, along with a couple of the tater tots and a fried egg. Add a dollop of the brown sauce and serve.

44

Cured pork belly kebab

With menemen sauce and a fried egg

Bacon and egg is an immutable combination. The menemen sauce and date glaze give this an exotic twist, and provide a subtler complement than ketchup.

600 g cured pork belly, sliced

FOR THE MENEMEN SAUCE
1 onion, finely diced
1 large red pepper, finely sliced
Olive oil
1 kg large vine tomatoes
30 g harissa paste

TO SERVE
Oil
4 eggs
4 Le Bab Flatbreads (see page 112)
1 handful of fresh chives, finely
   chopped

1. To make the menemen tomato sauce, fry the onion and red pepper in a little oil over a medium heat until golden brown. Blitz the tomatoes in a food processor until smooth, before adding to the pan and cooking over a low heat until all the excess liquid has evaporated and a thick sauce is left. Add the harissa and season.

2. Cook the pork slices on a barbecue or under a hot grill in the oven, turning halfway so that both sides are golden and crispy, for around 4 minutes.

3. Heat a frying pan with a little oil for a few minutes, before cracking the eggs into it. The hotter the pan, the crispier and lacier the bottom of the fried eggs will be.

4. Smooth a spoonful of the tomato sauce on the flatbreads, before topping with the grilled pork belly and the fried eggs, along with a scattering of chives.

Merguez kebab

With menemen sauce and a fried egg

The spicy lamb flavour of Merguez sausages makes a novel and interesting change to your brunch. It's still a delicious and uncomplicated combination for the first meal of the day.

600 g Merguez sausages

TO SERVE
Oil
4 eggs
1 portion of Menemen Sauce
  (see opposite)
4 Le Bab Flatbreads (see page 112)
1 handful of fresh chives, finely
  chopped

1. Cook the Merguez sausages on a barbecue or in a chargrill pan for around 5 minutes, turning halfway so that the sausages are crispy and cooked through.

2. Heat a frying pan with a little oil for a few minutes before cracking the eggs into it. The hotter the pan, the crispier and lacier the bottom of the fried eggs will be.

3. Smooth a spoonful of the menemen sauce on the flatbreads before topping with the sausages and the fried eggs, along with a scattering of chives.

Spring chicken kebabs

Grilled sprouting broccoli and harissa mayo

Big flavours abound in this gorgeously simple spring number. The broccoli gives a streak of crunchy acidity. Harissa mayo packs a smoky and fiery punch.

800 g skinned and boned chicken
  thighs

FOR THE CHICKEN SPICE

1 teaspoon cayenne powder

1 teaspoon ground cinnamon

½ teaspoon ground cloves

2 teaspoons ground coriander

1½ tablespoons ground cumin

½ teaspoon ground nutmeg

1 tablespoon freshly ground
  black pepper

½ teaspoon ground star anise

½ teaspoon ground turmeric

FOR THE HARISSA MAYONNAISE

15 g harissa paste

100 g Le Bab Mayonnaise
  (see page 116)

FOR THE PICKLED CHARRED SPROUTING BROCCOLI

500 g tenderstem broccoli

1 batch of Pickling Liquor (see
  page 119)

TO SERVE

4 Le Bab Flatbreads (see page 112)

1. Make the chicken spice mix by combining all the spices and mixing in a bowl. Dice the chicken into bite-sized chunks and rub with the spice mix before shaking off any excess and placing on a clean plate ready to cook. If you are cooking the chicken on a barbecue, you should skewer it onto four metal or wooden skewers.

2. Stir the harissa into the mayonnaise. Taste and add more if necessary, as harissa varies in strength.

3. Trim the hard bottoms off the broccoli stems and cook the broccoli on a hot barbecue or in a hot chargrill pan, turning often, until they are still crunchy but blackened in places. Put them in a sterilised kilner jar before boiling the pickling liquor and pouring over the broccoli (this will keep for 3 or 4 days in the fridge).

4. Season the chicken with salt and cook over a barbecue, turning frequently every 30 seconds, until cooked through. Alternatively, cook in a frying pan or chargrill pan over a medium heat for around 5 minutes.

5. Place the cooked chicken on the flatbreads before adding a couple of pieces of the pickled sprouting broccoli. Top with the harissa mayo and serve.

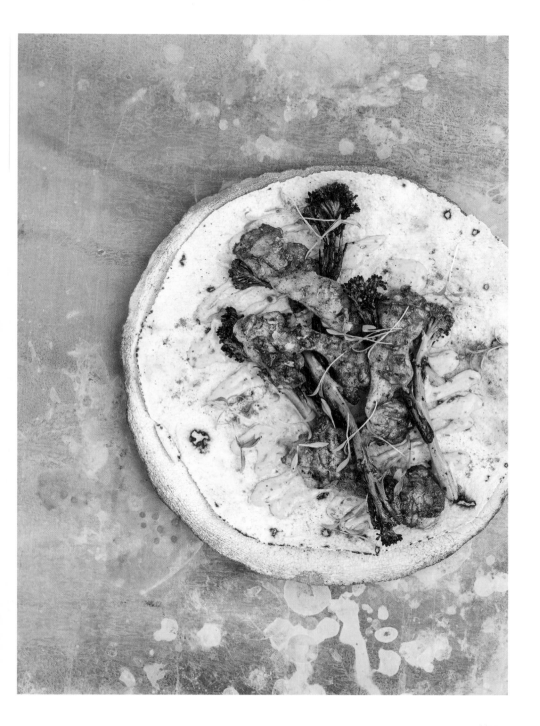

Halloumi kebabs

Deep-fried halloumi, mixed leaves, pear and cucumber

Everybody loves fried cheese! Halloumi adopts a lovely, stringy texture when deep-fried. Pear and cucumber provide the sweetness and freshness to cut across its salty flavour.

FOR THE HALLOUMI

15 g smoked paprika

80 g plain flour

4 eggs

100 g panko breadcrumbs

750 g halloumi, sliced into
   1–2 cm thick wedges

Oil, for frying

FOR THE SALAD

80 g mixed leaves

4 teaspoons olive oil

1 teaspoon white wine vinegar

TO SERVE

½ cucumber

Olive oil

4 Le Bab Flatbreads (see page 112)

150 g full-fat Greek yoghurt

1 pear, diced into 1 cm cubes

25 g fresh mint leaves

1. Slice the cucumber in quarters, scraping out the seeds with a spoon. Season with salt and toss in olive oil. In a hot chargrill pan or on the barbecue, char the cucumber batons until the skin is blackened, before removing from the heat and cutting into 1 cm cubes.

2. Mix the smoked paprika through the plain flour and put it in a bowl. In a separate bowl, beat the egg along with a teaspoon of water. In a third bowl, pour in the panko breadcrumbs. Toss the first wedge of halloumi in the plain flour, then dip it in the egg mix before finally dipping it in the breadcrumbs. Make sure the halloumi is totally covered in panko with no gaps. Repeat with the other slices.

3. Fry the breadcrumbed halloumi in oil at 180°C in a deep-fat fryer or in a high-sided pan until golden brown. Remove from the oil and drain on some paper towels.

4. To serve, dress the salad leaves with the oil, vinegar and a little salt, and place on the flatbreads. Top with a few dollops of yoghurt and the cubes of pear and cucumber. Finally, top with a few slices of the fried halloumi and a few mint leaves.

Slow-roasted goat's leg

With flatbreads and vegetables, salads or couscous

Goat's highly distinctive flavour is loved round the world, but not widely known in the UK. This is a truly unique, family-style centerpiece for the dinner table.

1 goat leg

FOR THE GOAT SPICE

2 teaspoons ground cumin

2 teaspoons garam masala

2 teaspoons ground black pepper

2 teaspoons ground coriander

1 teaspoon sumac

1 teaspoon cayenne pepper

1 teaspoon ground turmeric

1 teaspoon ground cinnamon

1 bay leaf

2 garlic cloves

50 g salt

TO SERVE

4 Le Bab Flatbreads (see page 112)

1. Season the goat leg heavily. Mix all the spices and rub the leg with them. Wrap the leg in tin foil and place it in the oven for a good 6–7 hours at 130°C/250°F/Gas mark 1.

2. Remove from the oven and and let the meat rest for 15 minutes before slicing. Serve with flatbreads and your choice of vegetables, couscous, salads or pickles.

Mackerel kebabs

Grilled mackerel fillet, lettuce, dill and pickled fennel salad

Serves 4

British mackerel has grown in popularity but is still an unsung hero. To our minds it is one of the finest fish available, with a beautiful fat content (it's also very high in omega-3) that's balanced with a zippy garnish.

4 mackerel fillets, with the skin left on

Olive oil

2 baby gem lettuces, ripped

FOR THE PICKLED FENNEL

1 fennel bulb

½ batch of Pickling Liquor (see page 119)

TO SERVE

4 Le Bab Flatbreads (see page 112)

15 g fresh dill sprigs

1. Quarter the fennel and remove the hard core. Slice the bulb lengthways, but not too thinly as you want a little bit of crunch still. Place the fennel in a sterilised kilner jar, then bring the pickling liquor to a boil and pour over the fennel slices. Allow to cool and ideally leave to infuse overnight to get enough of the fennel flavour into the vinegar.

2. Season the mackerel with salt and drizzle with olive oil before placing skin side down over a hot barbecue or in an extremely hot chargrill pan. If the skin sticks to the barbecue or pan, it is not hot enough. Cook for a minute or so, before flipping the fish fillets and cooking on the other side for another minute or two. Remove from the heat.

3. Dress the baby gem with a splash of olive oil and some of the cooled fennel pickling liquor. Arrange a few leaves on top of a flatbread, and add two of the mackerel fillets. Top with some of the pickled fennel slices and a few sprigs of dill.

Winter pork kebabs

Golden beetroot relish, pickled charred cabbage, dill mayo and crackling

Serves 4

2 pork tenderloins

FOR THE PORK SPICE

1 teaspoon ground cinnamon

½ teaspoon ground cloves

½ teaspoon ground coriander

½ teaspoon ground nutmeg

1 teaspoon freshly ground
black pepper

1 teaspoon ground turmeric

½ teaspoon fennel seeds

2 teaspoons ground cumin

FOR THE PICKLED CABBAGE

1 hispi or sweetheart cabbage

1 batch of Pickling Liquor
(see page 119)

2 teaspoons smoked paprika

FOR THE DILL MAYO

100 g Le Bab Mayonnaise
(see page 116)

15 g fresh dill, finely chopped

FOR THE GOLDEN BEETROOT RELISH

750 g peeled golden beetroots

75 ml white wine vinegar

25 g sugar

1 teaspoon salt

1 fresh red chilli

TO SERVE

4 Le Bab Flatbreads (see page 112)

1 bag store-bought pork scratchings

This kebab utilises a number of brilliant winter vegetables that go classically well with pork. It's evocative of South-Eastern European flavours.

1. All your spices for this should be ground, except for the fennel seeds, which should be whole. Mix them together in a bowl and add the whole tenderloins. Dust the pork well with the spices then shake off any excess. Place the pork on a tray ready to cook.

2. To make the pickled cabbage, quarter your cabbage, removing the hard heart, and slice widthways into chunky shreds. Throw these into an extremely hot chargrill pan (or preferably onto the barbecue if cooking over coals) and leave them for 2–3 minutes to char and blacken a little bit before putting the cabbage into a sterilised kilner jar. Boil the pickling liquor along with the smoked paprika, before pouring it whilst it's still hot over the cabbage (this will keep for up to a week in the fridge).

3. For the dill mayonnaise, mix the mayonnaise with the finely chopped fresh dill.

4. For the beetroot relish, combine the raw peeled beetroots with the vinegar, sugar, salt and chilli in a food processor and blitz to the consistency of wet couscous. This can be done in advance, however the beetroots will discolour over the course of a few hours (although the flavour won't be affected).

5. Cook the pork whole on the barbecue, turning the tenderloins every minute, wrap them and let them rest for 5 minutes more, slice and serve. If not possible, use a chargrill pan and cook for around 10 minutes in a medium heat, rest as you would for the barbecue

6. Spread a spoonful of the golden beetroot relish across each flatbread, before adding the pork slices. Top with dill mayo, some pickled cabbage and a few shards of crackling.

Grouse

Spatch cooked grouse served with aromatic pilaf rice and redcurrant glaze

2 wild grouse

FOR THE GROUSE SPICE

1 teaspoon black pepper

1 teaspoon green cardamom pods

FOR THE PILAF RICE

900 ml chicken stock (or follow the package instructions)

400 g long-grain brown rice

1 tablespoon ground coriander

20 g salt

FOR THE REDCURRANT GLAZE

50 ml chicken stock

50 g redcurrant jelly

TO SERVE

Watercress

The intense, gamey flavour of this renowned but rarely eaten bird is tempered by a delicately sweet redcurrant glaze, and complemented by the slight smokiness achieved by finishing on the grill.

1. Spatchcock the grouse by cutting down both sides of the backbone from the tail end to the neck (the backbone is on the flat underside). Spread the bird by placing it on a chopping board breast side up and pushing down until it's flattened. Turn the bird over and carefully cut out the cartilaginous breastbone. Grind the spices and rub the bird well with them.

2. To make the pilaf rice, add the ingredients together in a pan (the stock should be cold), give them a stir, cover and cook over a medium–low heat. The rice should take 12–15 minutes to absorb all the liquid. Have a taste – if it is not quite done, you can add a little more liquid and continue cooking for a bit longer. Alternatively, you can follow the package instructions. Check the rice for seasoning once it's cooked.

3. Season and place the grouse on a rack over a low heat on the barbecue, very gently cooking and keeping turning them every 30 seconds, for about 6 minutes, until they are cooked through. Alternatively cook in a frying pan or chargrill pan, turning often, over a medium heat for 7–8 minutes.

4. To make the redcurrant glaze, in a pan mix the stock and jelly together until the mixture becomes liquid but thick, brushing the birds once they come off the fire.

5. Place some rice on the bottom of a serving plate and the birds on top. Garnish with some seasoned watercress.

Aged dairy beef

With giant couscous, fresh hazelnut pesto and pickled chillies

Dairy beef has recently been causing a storm in the gastronomic community. In certain breeds, slow ageing on a grass-fed diet gives incredible depth of flavour and distribution of fat. We suggest rump for the meatiest flavour-but feel free to substitute your favourite cut.

FOR THE HAZELNUT PESTO

100 g hazelnuts

4 teaspoons olive oil

FOR THE COUSCOUS

2 shallots, diced

Vegetable oil

300 g giant couscous

500 ml chicken stock

A pinch of salt

FOR THE PICKLED CHILLIES

1 batch of Pickling Liquor (see page 119)

4 fresh red chillies

FOR THE DAIRY BEEF

1 kg rump steaks

1. Roast the hazelnuts at 165°C/320°F/Gas mark 3 for a good 10 minutes, turning them every now and then. Once roasted, allow them to cool, then blitz with the oil in a food processor until the mixture comes to a pesto-like consistency.

2. Sweat the shallots in a bit of oil, add the giant couscous, stir a little bit, and then add the stock and 150 ml water. Keep stirring until all the liquid is absorbed. Add extra if needed. Before serving, add the pesto – it will create a very creamy texture. Taste and season as required – the amount of salt needed will vary with the chicken stock used.

3. Boil the pickling liquor and pour over the chillies in a sterilised kilner jar (this will keep for a couple of weeks in the fridge).

4. Season and cook the steak on a chargrill pan over a high heat, flipping the meat every 30 seconds, for around 3 minutes, or cook it further if not done enough for your liking. Give it a good 3 minutes rest while you chargrill the drained pickled chillies. Slice it on to the couscous and top with a grilled pickled chilli.

Guinea fowl

Slow-cooked with grilled lettuce and roast cherry tomatoes

Hugely flavoursome guinea fowl is caressed by simple tomatoes and lettuce, so plentiful and delicious at the height of the British summer.

300 g on the vine cherry tomatoes

Oil

Smoked paprika

2 baby gem lettuces

4 guinea fowl supremes or breasts

Ground coriander

White wine vinegar

TO SERVE

4 Le Bab Flatbreads
(see page 112), warmed

100 g full-fat Greek yoghurt

Oregano

1. Place the cherry tomatoes on a non-stick baking tray. Sprinkle them with oil, salt and smoked paprika and roast them gently at 165°C/320°F/Gas mark 3 for about 12 minutes.

2. In the meantime, cut the baby gem lettuces in half. Grill them on a chargrill pan, centre half down, over a high heat with just a sprinkle of oil and salt for a couple of minutes until they get some brown colour. Set them aside.

3. Rub the supremes with a bit of ground coriander and salt and proceed to cook them over a high heat in a chargrill pan, skin side down first. After a couple of minutes when the skin has coloured, flip them, add a splash of vinegar to deglaze the chargrill pan and introduce it to the oven at the same temperature as the tomatoes for around 6 minutes. Take the pan out and let the guinea fowl rest for a good couple of minutes.

4. Plate the guinea fowl supremes with the tomatoes and lettuce as a garnish and the deglazed meat juices poured over. Accompany with the warmed flatbreads and a spoonful of the yoghurt mixed with a sprinkle of oregano.

Barnsley chop

With spiced potatoes and tamarind slaw

The Barnsley chop is a full cross section of the short saddle comprising two pieces of loin and two little pieces of fillet, with enormous flavour from its generous surrounding of fat. It works perfectly with the intense spice of Bombay potatoes and the sweet and sour tang of tamarind.

4 Barnsley chops

FOR THE YOGHURT MARINADE

2 garlic cloves, grated

3 cm piece of fresh ginger, grated

2 teaspoons tandoori masala

1 teaspoon cayenne pepper

1 teaspoon garam masala

1 teaspoon ground cloves

400 g full-fat Greek yoghurt

FOR THE SPICED POTATOES

800 g Jersey royal new potatoes or any waxy new potatoes

Vegetable oil

2 garlic cloves, grated

3 cm piece of fresh ginger, grated

Fresh coriander, to serve

FOR THE TAMARIND SLAW

200 g cabbage, shredded

20 g tamarind paste

20 g roasted peanuts

1. Mix the ingredients for the yoghurt marinade together. In a bowl, season and cover the chops with the spiced yoghurt and leave in the fridge for at least a couple of hours, and ideally overnight.

2. For the spiced potatoes, roast the new potatoes in a little oil for around 30 minutes at 160°C/315°F/Gas mark 2 until soft. Using the heel of your hand, gently crush them so that they don't break totally but are slightly flattened. This will help more surface to be exposed and be seasoned. Season and set aside.

3. Using some unflavoured vegetable oil, fry the garlic and ginger together until soft but not colouring. Add the roasted potatoes and fry all together before adding some fresh coriander on top.

4. For the tamarind slaw, mix all the slaw ingredients together and season well.

5. On a barbecue or in a hot chargrill pan, colour the outside of the chops before roasting in the oven at 170°C/325°F/Gas mark 3 for about 4–5 minutes. Allow to rest for 5 minutes before serving with the spiced potatoes and the tamarind slaw.

Turkey kebabs

Spiced cabbage, saffron mayo and spiced crumble

Serves 4

Use a top-quality, free-range turkey to ensure maximum flavour. Our most "Christmassy" kebab brings soft and sympathetic accompaniments to celebrate a much-maligned bird.

750 g turkey breast, diced

FOR THE TURKEY SPICE
½ teaspoon cayenne pepper
1 teaspoon ground cinnamon
½ teaspoon ground cloves
2 teaspoons ground coriander
2 teaspoons ground cumin
½ teaspoon ground nutmeg

FOR THE SPICED CABBAGE
500 g hispi or sweetheart cabbage
Olive oil
1 tablespoon garam masala

FOR THE SPICED CRUMBLE
100 g panko breadcrumbs
20 g pumpkin seeds
30 g roasted almonds, crushed

TO SERVE
Saffron
1 portion of Le Bab Mayonnaise
  (see page 116)
4 Le Bab Flatbreads (see page 112)

1. Combine all the turkey spices and mix in a bowl. Rub the turkey with the spice mix before shaking off any excess and placing on a clean plate, ready to cook.

2. For the spiced cabbage, quarter your cabbage and remove the tough core. Finely slice the quarters. In a large non-stick frying pan, fry the cabbage over a high heat with a little olive oil, the garam masala and some salt for around 5 minutes until slightly softened but still with some bite.

3. For the spiced crumble, toast the panko breadcrumbs and the pumpkin seeds over a medium heat until the panko gets golden. Mix with the roasted almonds and set aside.

4. Soak a pinch of saffron in a drizzle of water and gently warm it up for a minute. Set aside and let cool. When making your mayonnaise, add that water in at the end. The mayonnaise will turn orange.

5. Season the turkey with salt and cook over a barbecue, turning frequently every 30 seconds, until cooked through. Alternatively, cook in a frying pan or chargrill pan over a medium heat. This should take around 5 minutes.

6. Spread a little of the cabbage on your flat breads, place the turkey on top, drizzle with some saffron mayo and sprinkle a fair amount of the spiced crumble on top.

Pork shish kebab

Roasted broccoli tabbouleh, chermoula mayo, pickled kohlrabi and crackling

A Le Bab classic. Roasted broccoli offers a vegetable umami undercurrent to this spicy kebab with a great cross section of textures and flavours.

2 pork tenderloins

FOR THE PORK SPICE
2 teaspoons allspice
20 g garam masala
2 teaspoons cayenne pepper
2 teaspoons freshly ground
  black pepper
1 tablespoon ground turmeric

FOR THE CHERMOULA MAYO
20 g Le Bab Mayonnaise
  (see page 116)
100 g Le Bab Chermoula
  (see page 117)

FOR THE ROASTED BROCCOLI TABBOULEH
2 broccoli heads

FOR THE PICKLED KOHLRABI
2 kohlrabi
1 batch of Pickling Liquor
  (see page 119)

TO SERVE
5 Le Bab Flatbreads (see page 112)

1. Mix the pork spices together then rub the pork.

2. Combine the mayo and chermoula until homogeneously mixed.

3. To make the tabbouleh, cut the broccoli into florets, discarding the stem. Season and roast in the oven at 160°C/315°F/Gas mark 2 for around 10 minutes, then blitz in a food processor.

4. To make the pickled kohlrabi, slice the kohlrabi into 1 cm slices and grill them or use a chargrill pan until you can see marks on them, then cut into 1 cm chunks. Introduce them into a sterilised kilner jar. Boil the pickling liquor, and add to the kohlrabi.

5. Cook the tenderloins whole on the barbecue, turning them every minute for a good 8 minutes, then wrap them and let them rest for 5 minutes. Alternatively, use a chargrill pan and cook for around 10 minutes over a medium heat, rest as you would for the barbecue, then slice.

6. On a flatbread, place the pork slices, dress with the mayo and scatter with the pickled kohlrabi and the roasted broccoli tabbouleh.

Salmon tikka

Marinated grilled salmon, spiced basmati rice and raisin purée

An Indian-inspired kebab using a light marinade and gentle grilling to prepare a great British fish. The sweet raisin purée brightens the dish like a chutney served with curry.

800 g salmon fillet

100 g raisins

FOR THE SALMON MARINADE

100 g tomato purée

400 g full-fat Greek yoghurt

2 teaspoons cayenne pepper

4 teaspoons ground turmeric

35 g garam masala

FOR THE SPICED RICE

400 g basmati rice

2 teaspoons freshly ground
   black pepper

1 tablespoon ground coriander

20 g salt

TO SERVE

Fresh herbs such as
   corriander or rosemary

1. Cook the tomato purée in a frying pan over a low heat for about 5 minutes until it darkens slightly in colour. Allow to cool before mixing with the yoghurt, cayenne, turmeric and garam masala. Cut each salmon fillet into four or five chunks and rub all over generously with the marinade. Keep in the fridge until ready to use.

2. Simmer the raisins gently in just enough water to cover until the raisins are totally soft. Drain off the excess water and blend the raisins in a food processor until they form a smooth paste. Pass through a fine sieve.

3. To make the rice, add 1 litre cold water (or follow the package instructions) and the rest of the ingredients to a pot. Give it a nice mix, cover and cook over a medium–low heat for about 12–15 minutes or for as long as the package instructions recommend until the rice has absorbed all the liquid. Set aside.

4. Skewer the salmon, season and cook for around 4 minutes on the barbecue, turning regularly, until the salmon is almost cooked through, but still a little pink in the middle, then remove from the heat. Alternatively, you can cook the salmon in a non-stick frying pan over a low heat, turning every minute, for roughly the same time.

5. In a bowl, serve out a little of the spiced rice before topping with the salmon. Add a generous spoonful of the raisin purée around and top with the fresh herbs.

Octopus kebab

Grilled tentacles, salad and fried potatoes

Smoky but light, this simple seafood kebab is a perfect summer barbecue dish that will surprise and delight whoever you serve it to.

1.5 kg frozen octopus

FOR THE DRESSING
75 ml olive oil
20 ml white wine vinegar

FOR THE SALAD
2 baby gem lettuces
15 g fresh dill

TO SERVE
4 Le Bab Flatbreads (see page 112)
600 g potatoes
Oil, for frying
Smoked paprika

1. Leave the octopus overnight in the fridge to thaw. In a big pot, get well-seasoned water up to a simmer. Cook the octopus for about 30–35 minutes, making sure it does not boil, just gently simmer. Check with a spike – it should run through easily when cooked. Set aside and let it steam and chill. Cut the tentacles right up to the head – you need two per portion. Use the head to make the dressing.

2. To make the dressing, blitz the oil, vinegar and half of the cooked octopus head using a hand blender. Season to taste.

3. Dress the lettuce leaves with the octopus dressing, add the dill to taste and place on the flatbreads.

4. Peel the potatoes and cut them with a mandolin or using a knife to a very skinny shape. Deep fry them in oil until very crispy and season them with smoked paprika and salt. Top the kebabs with them.

5. In a non-stick pan, with a drizzle of oil and over a high heat, cook the tentacles. Season and colour as much as you can for around 3 minutes. Once they are crusty on the outside, dice them and place on top of the flatbreads, super skinny fries and salad.

Summer chicken kebab

Mixed leaves, pickled baby turnips, honey toum and Jersey royal crisps

Serves 4

800 g skinned and boned chicken
thighs, diced

FOR THE CHICKEN SPICE

1 tablespoon fresh black pepper

2 teaspoons ground coriander

1 teaspoon ground fenugreek

FOR THE PICKLED TURNIPS

10 baby turnips

½ batch of Pickling Liquor
(see page 119)

FOR THE HONEY TOUM

1 tablespoon honey

100 g Le Bab Toum (see page 119)

**FOR THE JERSEY ROYAL
CRISPS**

250 g Jersey royal new potatoes

Oil, for frying

2 teaspoons smoked paprika

FOR THE SALAD

2 teaspoons white wine vinegar

½ tablespoon honey

2 tablespoons olive oil

½ tablespoon ground fennel

½ tablespoon ground ginger

80 g mixed leaves

TO SERVE

4 Le Bab Flatbreads (see page 112)

The delicate flavours of this kebab are perfect for summer, and let the spicy barbecued chicken shine through. A touch of honey in the toum works brilliantly with the soft mixed leaves.

1. Combine the black pepper, coriander and fenugreek in a bowl and add the diced chicken thighs. Toss them in the spices and put to one side, ready to cook when all the other elements are prepared.

2. Slice the turnips to a 2 mm thickness before putting them into a sterilised kilner jar. Boil the pickling liquor and pour it whilst it's still hot over the turnip slices.

3. Add the honey to the toum and mix, being careful not to add too much honey as it can make the toum very runny.

4. Finely slice the new potatoes on a mandolin to about 1 mm thickness, before frying in oil at 160°C until golden. Toss the crisps whilst still hot from the oil in salt and smoked paprika and allow to cool.

5. To make the salad dressing, whisk together the vinegar, honey, oil, fennel and ginger and season to taste. Set aside.

6. Season the chicken with salt and cook over a barbecue, turning frequently every 30 seconds, until cooked through. Alternatively, cook in a frying pan or chargrill pan over a medium heat. This should take around 5 minutes.

7. When the chicken is cooked and you are ready to serve, dress the salad. Lay the leaves on the flatbreads before topping with the chicken, honey toum, pickled baby turnips and paprika crisps.

Barlotti bean falafel kebab

Mixed leaves, toum and pickled kale

The use of alternative pulses makes this a unique falafel, with more umami flavour. Its simple garnish packs a big flavour, and when the toum is made the traditional way (without egg white) it is 100% vegan.

FOR THE FALAFEL

250 g dried borlotti beans

2 teaspoons ground cumin

2 teaspoons ground coriander

½ teaspoon cayenne pepper

1 garlic clove

1 teaspoon salt

2 shallots, finely diced

2 teaspoons capers

15 g fresh coriander, chopped

Oil, for frying

FOR THE PICKLED KALE

1 batch of Pickling Liquor
  (see page 119)

200 g kale leaves, tough stems
  removed

1 fresh red chilli

TO SERVE

100 g mixed leaves

Olive oil

5 Le Bab Flatbreads (see page 112)

1 portion of Le Bab Chilli Sauce
  (see page 117)

1 portion of Le Bab Toum
  (see page 119)

1. The night before you want to make the falafel, soak the borlotti beans in plenty of water. The next morning, drain them and blend in a food processor along with the spices, garlic, salt and 75 ml water into a thick but relatively smooth paste. Pour the mix into a bowl and incorporate the diced shallots, capers and chopped coriander.

2. For the pickled kale, boil the pickling liquor and pour it over the kale leaves and chilli in a sterilised kilner jar. Once cool, it is ready to use (this will keep for a couple of weeks in the fridge).

3. Just before serving, shape the falafel with a dessert spoon or your hands and deep or shallow fry in some oil at 180°C for around 2–3 minutes until brown and crispy, making sure they are fully cooked through.

4. Dress the mixed leaves with a little olive oil and salt and lay on the flatbreads before placing about five or six falafel on top of each kebab. Dot the chilli sauce around, drizzle with the toum and top with a few leaves of the pickled kale.

Pork Adana kebab

Spiced cabbage and fried kale

Fried kale is an indulgent expression of this deep-flavoured brassica, to work alongside cabbage, its brassica relative. Delicious with the fatty pork.

1 kg pork mince

FOR THE PORK SPICE

2 teaspoons ground turmeric

2 teaspoons ground cumin

2 teaspoons chilli flakes

90 g sultanas

1 onion, finely diced

20 g chopped fresh coriander

20 g salt

FOR THE SPICED CABBAGE

500 g hispi or sweetheart cabbage

Olive oil

1 teaspoon ground cumin

½ teaspoon cayenne powder

FOR THE FRIED KALE

200 g kale leaves

Oil, for frying

TO SERVE

4 Le Bab Flatbreads (see page 112)

1 portion of Le Bab Mayonnaise
 (see page 116)

1. In a bowl, thoroughly mix together the pork mince and the pork spice ingredients. Fry a small portion of the mince in a pan, and check the seasoning. Divide the mince into four and shape into four sausages about as long as the diameter of your flatbreads. Put to one side, ready to cook.

2. For the spiced cabbage, quarter your cabbage and remove the tough core. Finely slice the quarters. In a large non-stick frying pan, fry the cabbage over a high heat with a little olive oil, the spices and some salt for around 5 minutes until slightly softened but still with some bite.

3. Fry the kale leaves for a couple of minutes at 180°C in some oil in a deep-fat fryer, being careful as the leaves will spit. Remove from the fryer and drain on some paper towels, before seasoning.

4. Grill the pork on a barbecue, turning often, until cooked through. Alternatively, you can cook the pork in an oven at 170°C/325°F/ Gas mark 3 for around 6–7 minutes.

5. On a flatbread, place some of the spiced cabbage and top with the pork adana. Drizzle with mayonnaise before topping with some of the crispy kale.

Lamb adana kebab

Shallot and parsley salad

This quick and fresh kebab is a staff favourite when something light but satisfying is needed during a break in a busy shift. Frequently devoured behind the scenes at Le Bab!

800 g lamb mince

FOR THE LAMB SPICE

2 teaspoons ground cumin

1 teaspoon biber or red chilli pepper paste

1 teaspoon sumac

1 small onion, finely diced

1 garlic clove, finely grated

2 tablespoons chopped fresh parsley leaves

2 tablespoons fresh thyme leaves

2 teaspoons soy sauce

FOR THE SALAD

100 g shallots

3 tomatoes

10 g fresh parsley leaves

Olive oil

TO SERVE

4 Le Bab Flatbreads (see page 112)

1 portion of Le Bab toum (see page 119)

Sliced baby radishes (optional)

Sliced cucumber (optional)

1. Spice the lamb by mixing the mince with the cumin, biber, sumac, onion, garlic, parsley, thyme and soy sauce thoroughly. Divide the spiced lamb into four equal balls and shape into sausages about as long as the diameter of your flatbreads. Put to one side, ready to cook when all your other elements are ready.

2. Peel the shallots and slice thinly lengthways. Cut the tomatoes into quarters and deseed them, then slice. Dress the tomatoes, shallots and parsley in a bowl with olive oil and season.

3. Season and cook the lamb on a barbecue, turning often, until cooked through but still a little pink in the middle. Alternatively use a chargrill pan. It should take about 5 minutes over a medium heat.

4. Place the lamb on the flatbreads, followed by the toum and as much tomato, shallot and parsley salad as you like. Top with some baby radishes and cucumber if you want.

Iskender chicken kebab

Tomato sauce and pickled kale

Serves 4

800 g chicken thighs, boned and
skinned

FOR THE CHICKEN SPICE

1 teaspoon cayenne pepper

1 teaspoon ground cinnamon

½ teaspoon ground cloves

2 teaspoons ground coriander

4 teaspoons ground cumin

½ teaspoon ground nutmeg

1 tablespoon fresh black pepper

½ teaspoon ground star anise

½ teaspoon ground turmeric

FOR THE PICKLED KALE

1 batch of Pickling Liquor (see
page 119)

200 g kale leaves, tough stems
removed

1 fresh red chilli

FOR THE TOMATO SAUCE

1 kg vine tomatoes

Olive oil

1 onion, finely diced

2 teaspoons garam masala

2 teaspoons ground cumin

2 teaspoons ground coriander

1½ tablespoons dried oregano

TO SERVE

4 Le Bab Flatbreads (see page 112)

1 portion of Le Bab Mayonnaise
(see page 116)

Fresh parsley leaves

A take on a classic Turkish kebab. We use kale as a hearty pickle, which brings a deep and slightly bitter quality to the dish, and contrasts well with the sweetness of the tomato sauce.

1. Make the chicken spice mix by combining all the spices and mixing in a bowl. Dice the chicken into large bite-sized chunks and rub with the spice mix before shaking off any excess and placing on a clean plate ready to cook. If you are cooking the chicken on a barbecue, you should skewer it onto four metal or wooden skewers. However, if you are cooking it in a pan or in the oven, there is no need.

2. Boil the pickling liquor and pour it over the kale leaves and chilli in a sterilised kilner jar. Once cool, it is ready to use (this will keep for a couple of weeks in the fridge).

3. To make the tomato sauce, blend the raw tomatoes in a food processor until smooth and liquid. Heat some olive oil in a pan and fry the onion until golden brown before adding the spices and cooking for a couple of minutes to release their flavours. Add the blitzed tomatoes, turn down the heat and gently simmer the sauce for around an hour until it is thick and all the excess water has evaporated. Season.

4. Season the chicken with salt and cook over a barbecue, turning frequently every 30 seconds, until cooked through. Alternatively, cook in a frying pan or chargrill pan over a medium heat. It should take about 5 minutes.

5. When the chicken is ready, spread a spoonful of the tomato sauce onto a flatbread and top with the chicken. Drizzle with mayonnaise and top with the pickled kale leaves and some parsley leaves too.

Rabbit leg

Grilled, with lentil ragú

A rustic dish, redolent of the Med – be careful with the cooking of the rabbit to avoid it becoming tough. Correctly done, it will be flavoursome and tender.

4 rabbit legs

40 g rose harissa paste

FOR THE LENTIL RAGÚ

3 shallots, finely sliced

Olive oil

20 g salt

2 teaspoons ground turmeric

2 teaspoons garam masala

350 g dried puy lentils

750 ml chicken stock

TO SERVE

Fresh coriander leaves

Lemon zest

1. Sweat the shallots in a little oil, add the salt and spices and cook for a further couple of minutes. Add the lentils and stock. Simmer until the lentils are cooked, adding more liquid if necessary. Correct the seasoning. The final consistency should be of a loose risotto.

2. Season and brush the rabbit legs with the harissa paste. Colour the rabbit legs in a pan on both sides over a medium heat. Transfer the pan to the oven at 150°C/300°F/Gas mark 2 for around 12 minutes until they are cooked through, flipping them every 3 minutes.

3. Pour the lentil ragú on to a deep plate, add the rabbit legs on top and garnish with coriander leaves and lemon zest.

Spiced beef kebab

Grilled diced beef, hollandaise, harissa and watercress

Anise and green chilli love beef, so we combined them in this kebab. The pepperiness of watercress alongside the chilli relish brings a vibrant accompaniment to smoky beef and rich hollandaise.

FOR THE BEEF FILLET

1 kg beef fillet

Allspice

FOR THE HARISSA HOLLANDAISE

1 portion of Worcestershire Hollandaise (see page 39), just swapping the Worcestershire sauce for 25 g harissa paste

TO SERVE

Watercress

5 Le Bab Flatbreads (see page 112)

1. Cut the beef fillet into 4 cm cubes, season with salt and black pepper and rub with the allspice. Cook the beef cubes over a high heat on the barbecue or using a chargrill pan until nicely coloured on all sides. Keep turning the beef every 30 seconds as it cooks so it doesn't burn on any side until it is cooked to your liking, about 3 minutes for rare, 4 minutes for medium rare, 5 minutes for medium. Take off the heat and leave to rest for a few minutes before serving.

2. Place some watercress on the flatbreads, top with the beef and drizzle with hollandaise.

Almost authentic lamb kebab

Charred tomatoes, shallots and crispy aubergine

800 g lamb mince

FOR THE LAMB SPICE

2 teaspoons ground cumin

1 teaspoon biber or red chilli
pepper paste

1 teaspoon sumac

1 small onion, finely diced

1 garlic clove, finely grated

2 tablespoons chopped fresh
parsley leaves

2 tablespoons fresh thyme leaves

2 teaspoons soy sauce

FOR THE CRISPY AUBERGINE

1 aubergine

Plain flour

Oil, for frying

**FOR THE CHARRED
TOMATOES AND SHALLOTS**

2 vine tomatoes

2 shallots

1 teaspoon sumac

Olive oil

TO SERVE

1 portion of Tomato Sauce
(see page 79)

4 Le Bab Flatbreads (see page 112)

1 portion of Le Bab Toum
(see page 119)

Fresh parsley leaves

Aubergine and tomatoes are not traditionally British ingredients, but they are now available in late summer from some excellent producers in the UK.

1. Spice the lamb by mixing the mince with the cumin, biber, sumac, onion, garlic, parsley, thyme and soy sauce thoroughly. Divide the spiced lamb into four equal balls and shape into sausages about as long as the diameter of your flatbreads. Put to one side, ready to cook when all your other elements are ready.

2. Meanwhile, for the crispy aubergine dice the aubergine into 2 cm cubes and put them in a bowl. Sprinkle with the salt and leave for half an hour, then drain off the excess water that the salt brings out of the aubergine. Pat the cubes dry, toss them in the flour and fry immediately at 160°C in a deep-fat fryer or in a high-sided pan for about 2–3 minutes. Once golden and crispy, remove from the oil onto some paper towels (there is no need to season since they have been salted).

3. For the charred tomatoes and shallots, slice the tomatoes in quarters and discard the seeds. Slice these quarters into segments about 1 cm thick. Slice the shallots into the same shape. Place everything onto a tray and season with salt and sumac before drizzling with oil. Using a blow torch or by placing under a grill in the oven, grill the tomatoes and shallots, turning, until charred and blistered.

4. Season and cook the lamb on a barbecue, turning often, until cooked through but still a little pink in the middle. This should take about 5 minutes over a medium heat. Alternatively, use a frying pan or chargrill pan.

5. Mix the aubergine cubes through the tomato sauce and smooth a spoonful onto a flatbread. Top with the lamb and drizzle over some toum. Balance a few of the charred tomato and shallot slices on top and garnish with some parsley leaves.

Roast vegetable kebab

Sprouting broccoli, cauliflower florets, harissa yoghurt and feta

Roasting brassicas, particularly broccoli and cauliflower, produces a deep and intense flavour. In this form, they're worthy of being the centre piece of a dish, and can balance the fragrant heat of the dressing.

400 g sprouting broccoli

400 g cauliflower florets

Harissa paste

Olive oil

FOR THE HARISSA YOGHURT

10 g harissa paste

100 g full-fat Greek yoghurt

TO SERVE

4 Le Bab Flatbreads (see page 112)

150 g Feta cheese

Cumin seeds

1. Trim the bottom of the broccoli stems and brush the broccoli and cauliflower with harissa. Place in a baking tray, season with salt, drizzle with olive oil and roast for around 15 minutes at 165°C/320°F/Gas mark 3 until a little soft and charred.

2. To make the harissa yoghurt, mix together the harissa paste with the yoghurt in a small bowl.

3. Top the flatbreads with a mixture of the broccoli and cauliflower before crumbling over the feta cheese, a dollop of harissa yoghurt and a sprinkle of cumin seeds.

Onglet

Maftoul risotto and herb yoghurt

Onglet is a lesser used steak which is flavoursome and tender when cooked correctly and sliced. In this dish, a gentle umami risotto of maftoul and a fresh herb yoghurt let the quality of the beef shine through.

1 kg onglet fillet

FOR THE SPICED MAFTOUL
1 onion, diced
Olive oil
400 g maftoul
2 teaspoons cumin seeds
2 teaspoons freshly ground black
  pepper
1 tablespoon ground coriander
20 g salt
300 ml chicken stock

FOR THE HERB YOGHURT
100 g full-fat Greek yoghurt
25 g fresh coriander leaves, chopped

1. Remove any excess sinew and connective tissue from the fillet or ask your butcher if you don't have time to do this yourself. Set it aside.

2. Cook the maftoul as if it were a risotto. Sweat the onions in a little olive oil until softened but not coloured then add the maftoul and spices and dry toast them for a minute. Add the salt, stock and 650ml of water, bring to the boil and then reduce the heat to a simmer until all the liquid has been absorbed – you may need to add more if the maftoul isn't quite cooked yet. Stir the maftoul regularly so that it doesn't catch on the bottom of the pan. Correct the seasoning once the maftoul is cooked.

3. Mix the yoghurt with the chopped coriander leaves.

4. Cook the onglet as a whole fillet. If you are using a barbeque, season the onglet and grill it over a high heat, turning it every 30 seconds. 2.5 minutes should be enough for rare, 3 minutes for medium rare and 4 minutes for medium. Alternatively you can cook it in a frying pan or chargrill pan over a medium heat for the same time. Let the steak rest for 3 minutes, then slice and serve over the maftoul, garnished with dollops of the herby yoghurt.

Squid kebab

Pickled shallots and chilli sauce

In the restaurant we serve this on a black flatbread (as pictured). Our Le Bab flatbreads work just as well, and the bold Mediterranean flavours of squid, parsley and chilli have a huge impact.

4 medium squid

FOR THE PERSILLADE

50 g fresh parsley leaves

2 garlic cloves

75 ml olive oil

Zest of 1 lemon

FOR THE PICKLED SHALLOTS

2 shallots, finely diced

100 ml vinegar

2 teaspoons ground turmeric

TO SERVE

80 g mixed leaves

Olive oil

4 Le Bab flatbreads (see page 112)

1 portion of Le Bab Chilli Sauce
 (see page 117)

1. Ask your fishmonger to prepare the squid. Chop the parsley roughly, grate the garlic and mix with the oil and lemon zest. Season the squid tubes and brush them with the herb mix.

2. Place the shallots in a small pan, pour over enough vinegar to cover, add the turmeric and season. Bring the vinegar to a boil over a medium heat, stirring regularly – keep a close eye on the shallots to avoid them burning on the bottom of the pan, they should become yellow. Set aside to cool.

3. If you are cooking the squid over a barbecue, make sure it is very hot. The squid will need approximately 1.5 minutes on each side as it will continue cooking gently with its own residual heat. Alternatively, you can use a chargrill pan or a frying pan over a high heat for the same amount of time. Once cooked, transfer the squid to a chopping board and slice into rings. Arrange the slices on top of some mixed leaves dressed with olive oil and salt on the flatbreads. Garnish with chilli sauce and the pickled shallots.

4. For a different experience, season the squid tentacles and dust them with flour. Shake off any excess and deep fry for a minute at 180°C, before adding to your kebab.

Summer lamb Adana

Harissa mayo and charred tomatoes and shallots

800 g lamb mince

FOR THE LAMB SPICE

2 teaspoons ground cumin

1 teaspoon biber or red chilli pepper paste

1 teaspoon sumac

1 small onion, finely diced

1 garlic clove, finely grated

2 tablespoons chopped fresh parsley leaves

3 tablespoons fresh thyme leaves

2 teaspoons soy sauce

FOR THE HARISSA MAYONNAISE

10 g harissa paste

100 g Le Bab Mayonnaise (see page 117)

FOR THE CHARRED TOMATOES AND SHALLOTS

2 large vine tomatoes

2 shallots

1 teaspoon sumac

Olive oil

TO SERVE

½ cucumber

4 Le Bab Flatbreads (see page 112)

Fresh parsley leaves

Summer brings ingredients that allow us to echo traditional Turkish combinations. Evocative of an authentic Turkish adana, using brilliant British produce: a classic combination with the unorthodox addition of chermoula from the Middle East.

1. Spice the lamb by mixing the mince with the cumin, biber, sumac, onion, garlic, parsley, thyme and soy sauce thoroughly. Divide the spiced lamb into four equal balls and shape into sausages about as long as the diameter of your flatbreads, ready to cook.

2. Stir the harissa into the mayonnaise.

3. For the charred tomatoes and shallots, quarter the tomatoes and remove the seeds. Cut them into strips and place on a baking tray. Peel the shallots, halve them and slice thinly before placing them on the same baking tray. Season both with the sumac, a pinch of salt and a splash of olive oil. With a blow torch or by placing under a hot grill in the oven, grill the tomatoes and shallots, turning, until charred and blistered.

4. Quarter the cucumber and remove the seeds with a spoon. Slice the cucumber into batons about 10 cm long.

5. Season and cook the lamb on a barbecue, turning often, until cooked through but still a little pink in the middle. Alternatively, you can use a frying pan or chargrill pan. It should take around 5 minutes over a medium heat.

6. Place each lamb adana on a flatbread and drizzle with harissa mayonnaise. Top with the charred slices of tomato and shallot, as well as a few batons of cucumber and some parsley leaves, to garnish.

Pig's head kebab

Braised and roasted, served with pickled vegetables

Le Bab's iconic sharing dish, made for meat lovers. The crispy skin and unctuous cheek meat form an irresistibly delicious combination, with the necessary and elevating contrast of crunchy, fresh pickled vegetables to cut across their rich meaty flavour.

½ pig's head

1 onion, roughly chopped

1 carrot, roughly chopped

2 sticks of celery, roughly chopped

1 tablespoon coriander seeds

1 teaspoon green cardamom pods

1 bay leaf

1 teaspoon whole cloves

1 teaspoon freshly ground black pepper

2 star anise

Pomegranate molasses (optional)

FOR THE SALADS

2 carrots, julienned

2 purple carrots, julienned

2 kohlrabi, julienned

4 shallots, halved and thinly sliced

1 tablespoon white wine vinegar

1 tablespoon olive oil

Sumac

TO SERVE

4–6 Le Bab Flatbreads (see page 112)

1. Ask your butcher for a whole pig's head, cut in half, with the brains removed. Put the halved head, along with the roughly chopped onion, carrot, celery and spices, in a deep stockpot and cover with water. Bring to the boil and simmer very gently for about 3½ hours to break down the collagen and tougher meats within the head. To test if it is cooked, poke a skewer into the pig's cheek – it should be totally soft. Let the head cool in the water before you carefully remove it, then keep it in the fridge, unwrapped, so the skin dries out. Reduce the cooking liquid until it is the thickness of gravy then pass through a very fine sieve and season.

2. Once the pig's head is totally cold, it is ready to be put in the oven at 240°C/475°F/Gas mark 8 for about 40 minutes to crisp up the skin. Remove from the oven when the skin is hard and crispy. Turn the head skin side down and remove the top and bottom jawbone. Discard the eyeball and any excess fat and shred the meaty bits. Cut the crackling into strips. Season both.

3. To assemble the accompanying salads, place the two types of carrot and the kohlrabi in one bowl and the sliced shallots in another. Just before serving, dress both bowls with the white wine vinegar, olive oil and a pinch of salt, and give the shallots an extra pinch of sumac as well.

4. Serve the pig's head meat and crackling with the two salads, some warmed flatbreads and a jug of the hot gravy for people to help themselves to. We recommend adding a final touch of pomegranate molasses to the gravy just before serving.

Lobster kebab

Smoked corn mayo, grilled lobster, charred lettuce and pickled tomatoes

Our lobster kebab is one of our favourites, and just sings of summer. The light and fresh garnish complements the lobster without overwhelming its sweet, delicate flavour. Use a native lobster in the height of summer for the best value and quality.

4 whole lobsters

FOR THE SMOKED CORN MAYONNAISE

2 sweetcorn, in their husks

150 g Le Bab mayonnaise (see page 116)

FOR THE PICKLED TOMATOES

20 cherry tomatoes

100 ml white wine vinegar

25 ml sherry

FOR THE CHARRED LETTUCE

2 baby gem lettuces, quartered

Olive oil

Fresh lemon juice

TO SERVE

4 Le Bab Flatbreads (see page 112)

1. You can either buy prepared raw lobster, already shelled and usually frozen, or alternatively you can buy them live and prepare them yourself. If you decide to do so, bring a large pot of salted water to a rolling boil. Make sure there is enough water to fully submerge the lobsters – you may need to cook them in batches. To kill the lobsters humanely you can either put them in the freezer for 15 minutes before blanching them, or else run a knife through their heads lengthways, starting with the tip at the base of the head where it joins the body. Plunge the lobsters into the boiling water for 30 seconds and then straight into iced water to halt the cooking process. Once chilled, twist the head and claws off. Return the claws to the boiling water to cook for a further 5 minutes before plunging them once more into the iced water. To remove the tail meat, roll the tail onto its side and with the heel of your hand gently crush it until it cracks down the middle. Gently peel it away to obtain the tail intact – you can use the handle of a spoon to help ease the flesh away from the shell, especially where the segments join one another. For the claws, use the back of a heavy knife like a hammer to crack them. Take your time and be delicate!

2. To make the smoked corn mayonnaise char the outer husks of your sweetcorn until they darken and the corn is cooked through, ideally on a barbecue or else an extremely hot chargrill pan. Remove from the heat, peel off these blackened husks from the cooked part of the sweetcorn and cut off the kernels. Discard the husks and cores. In a food processor, blitz most of the sweetcorn kernels into a rough paste, saving a few to garnish, and season before stirring through the mayonnaise.

3. To make the pickled tomatoes, cut the cherry tomatoes in half and let them infuse in the white wine vinegar and sherry.

4. We strongly suggest cooking the lobster on a barbecue, over a low heat. Skewer the tails lengthways and season them. They will need 4–5 minutes of gentle cooking. You can also reheat the claws on the barbecue at the same time. Alternatively, you can use a chargrill pan on a medium heat. Colour the lobster on both sides then stand it up to colour the broad end of the tail too. Reduce the heat to a low flame and gently finish cooking the tails, approximately 4–5 minutes. Allow to rest for a minute or two before serving.

5. To prepare the lettuce, drizzle each quarter with a little olive oil and season. Grill over a high heat on the barbecue or else in a chargrill pan until they are slightly wilted and a little charred. Dress with a little more olive and some lemon juice.

6. To serve, smear a spoonful of smoked corn mayonnaise on each flatbread before topping with two pieces of charred lettuce, a lobster tail and its claws. Top with 5 or 6 pickled tomatoes and scatter over a few of the reserved charred corn kernels. Serve immediately.

Aubergine sabich

Pickled kale, charred tomatoes and crispy aubergine

Serves 4

Late summer vegetables shine through here. It balances the richness of the aubergine and toum with the acidity and piquancy of tomatoes and pickled kale.

FOR THE PICKLED KALE

1 batch of Pickling Liquor
(see page 119)

200 g kale leaves, tough stems
removed

1 fresh red chilli

FOR THE CHARRED TOMATOES

2 large vine tomatoes

Sumac

Olive oil

FOR THE CRISPY AUBERGINE

2 aubergines

Plain flour

Oil, for frying

TO SERVE

25 g whole blanched almonds

4 Le Bab Flatbreads (see page 112)

1 portion of Le Bab Toum
(see page 119)

1. To make the pickled kale, boil the pickling liquor, pour it over the kale leaves and chilli in a sterilised kilner jar. Once cool, it is ready to use (this will keep for a couple of weeks in the fridge).

2. Toast the almonds in the oven at 170°C/325°F/Gas mark 3 for 10 minutes until golden. Remove from the oven and crush.

3. For the charred tomatoes, slice the tomatoes into quarters and discard the seeds. Slice these quarters into segments about 1 cm thick. Season with salt and sumac before drizzling with oil. Using a blow torch or by placing under a hot grill in the oven, grill the tomatoes, turning once, until charred and blistered.

4. For the crispy aubergine, cut the aubergines into 3 cm cubes and put them in a bowl. Sprinkle over some salt and leave for 10 minutes until some water is released from the aubergines. Pat the cubes dry, dust with plain flour and shake off any excess. Deep or shallow fry the aubergines at 160°C for about 3 minutes or until they are golden. Remove from the oil onto some paper towels to drain (there is no need to season since they have already been salted).

5. On a flatbread, lay some of the just-fried aubergine chunks and top with toum. Scatter with the charred tomatoes and pickled kale, then top with crushed and roasted almonds.

Lentil falafel kebab

Falafel, roasted spiced carrots, yoghurt and leaves

Serves 4

This is a spicy, hearty winter dish. Carrots bring subtle sweetness that works naturally with the meaty flavour of lentils.

FOR THE LENTIL FALAFEL

250 g dried puy lentils

1 garlic clove

15 g salt

1 teaspoon cayenne pepper

2 teaspoons ground cumin

2 teaspoons ground coriander

Oil, for frying

FOR THE CHARRED SHALLOTS

2 shallots

1 teaspoon sumac

Olive oil

FOR THE SPICED ROASTED CARROTS

50 g butter

2 carrots, diced

1 whole star anise

2 green cardamom pods

TO SERVE

4 Le Bab Flatbreads (see page 112)

80 g mixed leaves

100 g full-fat Greek yoghurt

1. Soak the lentils overnight – they will double up in weight. In a food processor, blitz them into a smoothish paste with the garlic, salt, spices and 50 ml water. Shape the falafel with your hands into discs and lay them on a sheet of baking parchment.

2. To make the charred shallots, slice the shallots thinly before seasoning them with salt and the sumac and drizzling with oil. Using a blowtorch or by placing under a hot grill in the oven, grill the shallots until charred and blistered, turning once.

3. To make the spiced roasted carrots, melt the butter in a small pan before adding the diced carrot, spices and some salt. Fry over a low heat for about 15–20 minutes until the carrot is softened and slightly coloured.

4. When you're ready to serve, deep or shallow fry the falafel in some oil at 180°C until brown and crispy. On a flatbread, lay the leaves and charred shallots before topping with 5 or 6 pieces of falafel. Scatter over the spiced carrots and add generous dollops of the yoghurt.

Winter chicken kebabs

Hummus, toum, chilli sauce and pickled carrots

800 g skinned and boned chicken thighs

FOR THE CHICKEN SPICE

1 teaspoon cayenne pepper

1 teaspoon ground cinnamon

½ teaspoon ground cloves

2 teaspoons ground coriander

1½ tablespoons ground cumin

½ teaspoon ground nutmeg

1 tablespoon fresh black pepper

½ teaspoon ground star anise

½ teaspoon ground turmeric

FOR THE PICKLED CARROTS

1 carrot

1 purple carrot

½ batch of Pickling Liquor (see page 119)

FOR THE SQUASH HUMMUS

½ butternut squash, peeled, deseeded and diced

Olive oil

100 g chickpeas (in brine)

2 teaspoons fresh lemon juice

20 g tahini

1 garlic clove

TO SERVE

4 Le Bab Flatbreads (see page 112)

1 portion of Le Bab Toum (see page 119)

1 portion of Le Bab Chilli Sauce (see page 117)

One of our earliest ever kebabs. Pickled carrots brighten this kebab even in the middle of winter. The hummus brings a warm, gently sweet undertone.

1. Combine all the spices for the chicken in a bowl. Dice the chicken into bite-sized chunks and rub with the spice mix, before shaking off any excess and placing on a clean plate ready to cook.

2. To make the pickled carrots, first peel the carrots and discard their skin. Continue using a peeler to cut the rest of the carrot into long ribbons. Place these into a sterilised kilner jar. Heat the pickle liquor to dissolve the sugar then allow to cool completely before pouring over the carrots – if the liquor is too hot, the carrots will lose their crunch. N.B. If you are using purple and orange carrots pickle them separately otherwise the colour of the purple carrots will run.

3. To make the squash hummus, season the diced squash with salt and roast in an oven at 160°C/315°F/Gas mark 2 with a little olive oil for around 30–40 minutes until soft. Blend into a smooth paste, adding some water if it is too thick to purée, and put to one side. Drain the tin of chickpeas and add them to a food processor along with 1 tablespoon olive oil, 3 tablespoons water, the lemon juice, tahini, garlic and some salt. Blend until smooth, again adding some water if it gets too thick. Mix the hummus with the butternut squash purée and check the seasoning.

4. Season the chicken with salt and cook over a barbecue, turning frequently, every 30 seconds until cooked through. Alternatively, cook in a frying pan or chargrill pan over a medium heat for around 5 minutes.

5. Spread a little of the butternut squash hummus on the flatbreads, before adding the chicken pieces. Top with toum, some dots of chilli sauce and a few ribbons of the drained, pickled carrot.

Monkfish

Spiced monkfish tail, celeriac purée and caper salad

Monkfish is a meaty and distinctive fish, able to stand up to the smoke of the grill, the piquant salad and the rich flavour of celeriac. This is a blinder that will leave you gnawing at the bone.

1.8–2 kg whole monkfish tail

25g curry powder

FOR THE CELERIAC PURÉE

1 celeriac

50 g butter

200 ml whole milk

1 teaspoon curry powder

FOR THE SALAD

50 g fresh parsley, leaves picked

2 shallots, thinly sliced

30 g capers

Olive oil

TO SERVE

4 Le Bab Flatbreads (see page 112), warmed

1. To make the purée, peel the celeriac and roughly dice it into cubes. Melt butter in a pan over a medium heat, add the celeriac and gently fry for 3–4 minutes until lightly coloured. Add the milk and curry powder and simmer until the celeriac is soft. Blitz in a food processor then season.

2. Rub the monkfish tail with the curry powder and dust off any excess. Season and cook on a barbecue over a medium heat for 12 minutes, turning halfway through. Alternatively you can roast the monkfish in the oven at 160°C/310°F/Gas mark 3 for 10 minutes, then take it out, increase the temperature of the oven to 240°C/475°F/Gas mark 9, Gas Mark 8 and return the fish to the oven for a further 5 minutes to caramelise deeply. When cooked through, cover the monkfish with tin foil and leave to rest for 5 minutes as you would a joint of meat. Once rested, run a knife down either side of the spine – if it is cooked, the meat will come away without any resistance.

3. Mix together the parsley, shallots and capers. Dress with a little oil and season. Reheat the purée and place in a bowl. Serve the monkfish alongside the salad, celeriac purée and the warmed flatbreads.

Venison adana kebab

Blackberry and chilli jam, cavolo nero kimchi and artichoke crisps

Serves 4

The combination of venison and fermented cavolo nero is big and powerful. These strong flavours are tempered and balanced by the sweet blackberry preserve and Jerusalem artichoke. A kebab for game lovers.

800 g venison mince

1 onion, diced

FOR THE VENISON SPICE

2 teaspoons freshly ground
  black pepper

1 tablespoon allspice

1 tablespoon juniper berries

FOR THE FERMENTED
CAVOLO NERO

500 g cavolo nero

2 teaspoons salt

60 g shallots, finely chopped

3 garlic cloves, finely chopped

FOR THE BLACKBERRY
CHILLI JAM

500 g frozen blackberries

50 g sugar

1 tablespoon chilli flakes

FOR THE JERUSALEM
ARTICHOKE CRISPS

6 Jerusalem artichokes

Oil, for frying

TO SERVE

1 portion of Le Bab Mayonnaise
  (see page 116)

4 Le Bab Flatbreads (see page 112)

1. For the fermented cavolo nero, strip the leaves from their stems and chop roughly. Place them in a bowl, sprinkle with the salt, cover and leave in a warm place overnight. The salt will draw out some of the moisture from the leaves. The following day, brush off the salt, add the finely chopped shallots and garlic and place in a sterilised kilner jar. Leave for at least two nights, but ideally for a week or two, to ferment.

2. Combine the venison spices and mix them thoroughly with the venison mince and diced onions. Divide into four equal-sized balls and shape into sausages about as long as the diameter of your flatbreads.

3. To make the jam, simmer the frozen blackberries and sugar in a pan over a low heat until all the excess liquid has evaporated away and you have a thick, jam-like consistency. Remove from the heat, add the chilli flakes and pour into a sterilised kilner jar to cool (this will keep for up to a week in the fridge).

4. Slice the Jerusalem artichokes with a mandolin into 2 mm thick discs directly into some cold water with a squeeze of lemon juice to stop them discolouring. Drain the slices and then fry in oil at 160°C until golden and crispy, approximately 4 minutes. Drain on kitchen towels and season with salt while still hot.

5. Skewer the venison sausages and season with salt. Cook on the barbecue, turning every minute, for around 5 minutes until cooked through but still pink in the middle. Alternatively, you can cook the meat on a chargrill pan for approximately the same time.

6. Smear a dessertspoon of the jam on the flatbreads and place the venison adana on top. Drizzle with the mayo and top with the drained fermented cavolo nero and a handful of artichoke crisps.

Paneer kebab

Beetroot purée, pickled chard and crispy shallot rings

Serves 4

Our paneer kebab is our most recognised vegetarian dish, enjoyed by vegetarians and meat eaters alike. It has a great range of textures and flavours that interplay so wonderfully, underpinned by a purée inspired by Keralan beetroot thoran.

500 g paneer (shop-bought)

FOR THE PANEER MARINADE
200 g full-fat Greek yoghurt
50 g tomato purée
2 teaspoons cayenne pepper
2 teaspoons ground turmeric
15 g garam masala

FOR THE BEETROOT PURÉE
200 g beetroots
15 g desiccated coconut

FOR THE PICKLED CHARD
2 chard, leaves removed and
   stems reserved
½ batch of Pickling Liquor
   (see page 119)

FOR THE CRISPY SHALLOTS
4 shallots
100 g plain flour
Oil, for frying

FOR THE MAYONNAISE
4 teaspoons curry powder
100 g Le Bab Mayonnaise
   (see page 116)

TO SERVE
4 Le Bab Flatbreads (see page 112)
Fresh coriander leaves

1. Mix together the yoghurt and tomato purée, before stirring in the spices. Cut each pack of paneer into 12 equal-sized cubes and generously coat in the yoghurt mix. Leave to marinate for at least a couple of hours if possible.

2. Steam the beetroots in their skins for an hour or so until soft and tender. Let them cool a little before peeling the skins away with your fingers. If they've been cooked enough, the skins should slip away easily. Alternatively, you can buy ready-cooked beetroots, although the flavour won't be as good. When peeled, blitz the beetroots in a food processor with a little water and a good couple of pinches of salt until you have a smooth purée. Stir in the desiccated coconut.

3. To make the pickled chard, slice the white stems of the chard into matchsticks about 5 cm long and put them into a sterilised kilner jar. Bring the pickling liquor to the boil and pour it over the chard stems.

4. Slice the shallots into 3 mm thick discs, separating each disc into rings. Place these in water, separating each shallot ring as you do so. Drain the rings and toss them in flour before frying in oil at 180°C in a deep-fat fryer or in a high-sided pan and draining on paper towels.

5. Mix the curry powder through the mayonnaise. Skewer six pieces of paneer onto each of four skewers, season and cook on the barbecue until the cheese is coloured and soft and squidgy, approximately 4 minutes. Alternatively, you can cook them in an oven at 170°C/325°F/Gas mark 3 for around 5 minutes until the cheese is soft.

6. Smear some beetroot purée on a flatbread, before adding the cheese cubes, then a few pieces of the pickled and drained chard. Squeeze over the curry mayo and top with the crispy shallots and some coriander leaves.

Winter lamb adana kebab

Parsnip purée, parsnip crisps, curried mayo and pickled onions

Serves 4

800 g lamb mince

FOR THE LAMB SPICE

2 teaspoons ground cumin

1 teaspoon biber or red chilli
pepper paste

1 teaspoon sumac

1 onion, finely diced

1 garlic clove, finely grated

2 tablespoons chopped parsley

3 tablespoons fresh thyme leaves

2 teaspoons soy sauce

FOR THE PICKLED ONIONS

1 onion

Oil

½ batch of Pickling Liquor
(see page 119)

**FOR THE CURRY
MAYONNAISE**

2 teaspoons curry powder

100 g Le Bab Mayonnaise
(see page 116)

FOR THE PARSNIP CRISPS

3 parsnips

Oil, for frying

FOR THE PARSNIP PURÉE

25 g butter

2 teaspoons curry powder

500 ml whole milk

TO SERVE

4 Le Bab Flatbreads (see page 112)

This utilises a great British root in two ways. Pickled onions cut across the meaty lamb and the velvety richness of the parsnip purée.

1. Combine the mince with all of the spice mix ingredients. Divide the lamb into four equal-sized balls and shape into sausages roughly the width of your flatbreads. Set aside.

2. For the pickled onions, peel, top, tail and quarter the onion. Halve widthways and separate the layers into 'petals'. Lay these out in a single layer on a baking tray, cover with salt and a little olive oil and use a blow torch or hot grill to char until blackened. Place into a sterilised jar. Boil the pickling liquor and pour over the onion.

3. Mix the curry powder with the mayonnaise, tasting as you go!

4. Peel the parsnips of their outer layer and discard before continuing to peel the parsnips down to the core until you have a pile of long ribbons and the parsnip 'cores'. Deep or shallow fry the ribbons in oil at around 160°C until golden and crispy, then season. The cores will be used for the curried parsnip purée.

5. Slice the leftover parsnip into rough 1 cm cubes and fry in the butter for a few minutes, along with the curry powder. Add the milk and cook over a low heat for about 30 minutes until the parsnip is soft. Drain the softened parsnip, reserving the milk, and blitz in a food processor using some of the milk and a little water, to loosen, until you have a relatively thick, smooth purée. Season to taste.

6. Season and cook the lamb on a barbecue, turning often, until cooked but still a little pink in the middle. Alternatively use a frying or chargrill pan. It should take around 5 minutes over a medium heat.

7. Smooth a spoonful of the parsnip purée onto each flatbread and place the lamb on top. Scatter over the onion petals, before adding the curry mayo and a handful of parsnip crisps.

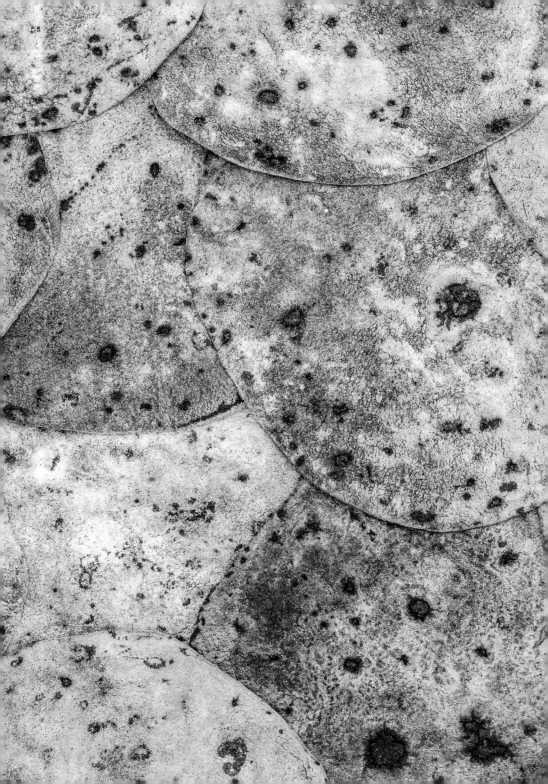

Basics

Le Bab flatbreads

560 g strong white flour
100 g strong wholemeal flour
20 g salt
2 teaspoons olive oil

1. Use a kneading machine/stand mixer for this recipe, although it can be done by hand applying some extra effort. Mix the dry ingredients together first, add 350 ml water slowly and then let it knead for a good 10 minutes at medium speed. Add the olive oil to shorten the dough and help it become more elastic, then let it combine and knead for a further 3–4 minutes.

2. Portion every flatbread into roughly 50 g each mini balls. Roll them out with a rolling pin (or use a pasta machine) very thinly and cook them individually in a non-stick frying pan, on a high heat, for around 8 seconds the first side and a bit less the second side. Keep them covered. Once you have piled up a few, wrap them up in cling film to avoid drying out. It is best to use these within a day, although if properly wrapped you may freeze them.

Tip

If you find that the dough is too sticky, use some flour during the rolling process.

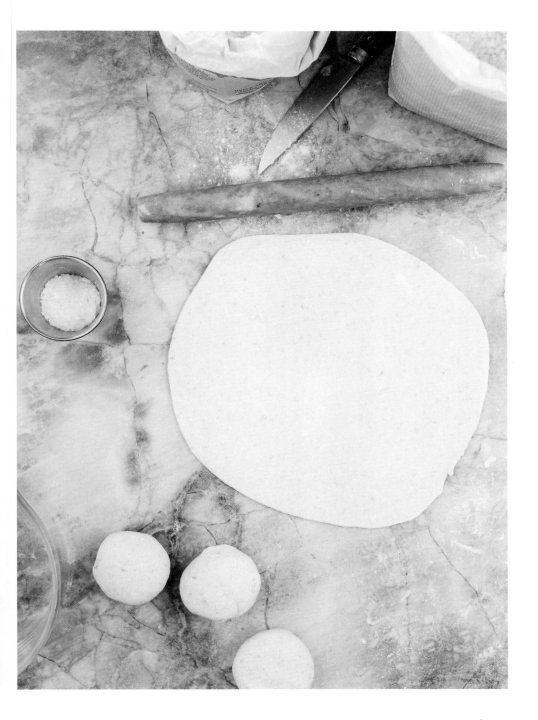

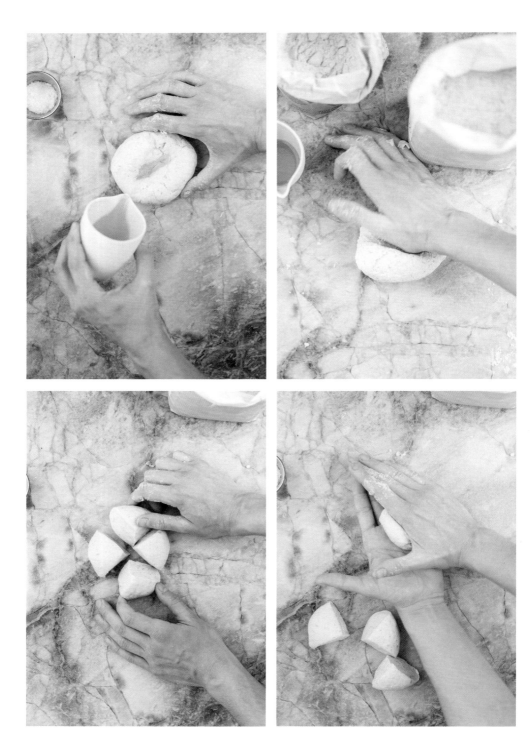

Green chilli relish

10 fresh green chillies
5 garlic cloves
2 teaspoons vegetable oil
25 g fresh coriander

1. Deseed and finely chop all of the chillies. Now finely chop the garlic. In a non-stick frying pan, heat up the vegetable oil over a low heat. Add the garlic and once the garlic has started to cook and soften, then add the chilli. Season and keep stirring until soft, then chop the coriander and add it to the rest. Mix and chill. This will keep in the refrigerator for a week in an airtight container.

Le Bab mayonnaise

1 whole egg
2 teaspoons Dijon mustard
2 teaspoons white wine vinegar
500 ml vegetable oil

1. In a food processor or with an electric whisk, beat together the egg, mustard and white wine vinegar until combined.

2. Pour the vegetable oil into the egg mix as slowly as possible, continuing to whisk (or whilst leaving the food processor on, if you are using that). Make sure that the oil isn't sitting on top of the egg, or not mixing in properly, as this will make the mayonnaise split. If your mayo is looking too thick, whisk in a little water. Keep going until all the oil is incorporated into the egg then season. You can store this in the fridge and use within 3 days.

Le Bab chermoula

50 g fresh parsley
50 g fresh coriander
5 fresh green chillies
4 garlic cloves
2 teaspoons white wine vinegar
1 tablespoon extra virgin olive oil
5 teaspoons ground cumin
4 teaspoons ground paprika

1. Combine all the ingredients in a food processor and blitz to form a paste. Season with salt. You may keep the chermoula in an airtight container for 3–4 days in the fridge, although we recommend to use it fresh.

Le Bab chilli sauce

Serves 5

400 g red chillies
5 garlic cloves
20 g tomato paste
20 ml olive oil
Juice of ½ lemon

1. On a barbecue or under the grill in the oven, grill the chillies and whole unpeeled garlic bulb, turning, until blistered and blackened. Place the blistered chillies and garlic on a roasting tray and wrap with tin foil. Cook at 150°C/300°F/Gas mark 2 for about 30 minutes until thoroughly cooked through and soft.

2. Remove the stalks from the chillies and squeeze the inside of the garlic out. In a food processor, blend the chillies and garlic along with the other ingredients into a smooth paste, then season to taste. You can keep this sauce for up to a week in the fridge.

Le Bab toum

1 egg white
1 garlic clove, finely grated
500 ml vegetable oil
2 teaspoons white wine vinegar

1. In a food processor or with an electric whisk, beat together the egg whites and finely grated garlic clove.

2. Once fully combined, slowly trickle in the vegetable oil whilst still whisking (or with the food processor on, if you are using that). Make sure that the vegetable oil is mixing in. If the toum gets too thick (which it will) add a dash of water to loosen it before adding the rest of the oil. When all the oil and a few splashes of water have been added, add the vinegar to stabilise the emulsion. Season. Keep in the fridge and use within 3 days.

Pickling liquor

500 ml white wine vinegar
50 g sugar
1 teaspoon salt

1. Place all the ingredients in a saucepan and bring to a boil. The salt and sugar will dissolve. Immediately pour the liquor into a sterilised kilner jar containing your chosen vegetables and leave to pickle.

Cocktails

The old bitter Alex

25 ml bourbon

35 ml vermouth rouge

20 ml fresh lemon juice

10 ml agave syrup

3 dashes of Angostura bitters

Maraschino cherry and a twisted
orange peel, to garnish

1. Add the bourbon, vermouth, lemon juice, agave and some cubed ice into a shaker. Shake well until cold then double-strain the mixture into a chilled old-fashioned glass full of cubed ice. Drop 3 dashes of Angostura bitters on top and, to finish, garnish with a maraschino cherry on a cocktail stick and a twisted orange peel.

The smokey sour

25 ml Laphroaig whisky

25 ml mezcal

25 ml fresh lemon juice

15 ml egg white

1 teaspoon maple syrup

3 dashes of Angostura bitters

1 maraschino cherry, to garnish

1. Add the Laphroaig, mezcal, lemon juice, egg white, maple syrup and ice into a shaker. Shake until cold then double-strain into a chilled old-fashioned glass full of cubed ice. Drop in 3 dashes of Angostura bitters and to finish garnish with a maraschino cherry on a cocktail stick.

The yellow rose-marine

1 bunch of fresh rosemary

Vodka

20 ml gin

20 ml fresh lemon juice

25 ml pineapple juice

15 ml agave syrup

A pinch of salt

1. Add a bunch of rosemary and vodka to a large sealable jar and allow to infuse. For the best success, leave it in a cool place for at least 3 days. Simply remove the sprigs before using, reserving one for this recipe.

2. Add 25 ml of the rosemary-infused vodka, the gin, lemon juice, pineapple juice, agave syrup, a pinch of salt and some ice into a cocktail shaker. Shake until cold then double-strain into a chilled martini glass.

3. Lightly burn a sprig of the rosemary over an open flame and use it as a garnish. Serve the drink while the rosemary is still smoking.

The sweet baby Burrough

50 ml ruby reserve port

20 ml dark rum

20 ml fresh lemon juice

½ teaspoon ground cinnamon

15 ml agave syrup

3 dashes of orange bitters

1 piece of orange peel and 1 maraschino cherry, to garnish

1. Add the port, rum, lemon juice, cinnamon, agave syrup, orange bitters and cubed ice to a shaker. Shake until cold and then double-strain the mixture into a chilled old-fashioned glass filled with cubed ice. Cut a piece of orange peel about the size of your thumb and hold it between your finger and thumb over the glass. Quickly bend the orange peel so the oil from the skin settles on the surface of the drink. Drop the orange peel into the drink and stir. To finish, garnish with a maraschino cherry on a cocktail stick.

The Mediterranean mermaid

220 g sugar

2 bunches of fresh mint

2 slices of cucumber

50 ml mastiha liqueur

25 ml Chartreuse

25 ml fresh lime juice

A pinch of salt

1 sprig of fresh mint, to garnish
(optional)

1. Combine 250 ml water and the sugar in a saucepan and bring to a boil, stirring until the sugar dissolves to make a sugar syrup.

2. Separate the mint leaves from the stems and, in another pan, boil the mint leaves for 10 seconds, then move them to iced water immediately to stop the cooking process. Separate the leaves and squeeze out all the water. Blitz the leaves with the sugar syrup and strain through muslin or cheesecloth. Keep in the fridge.

3. Muddle the cucumber slices in a shaker, pour in all the other ingredients along with 20 ml of the mint syrup, shake well and double-strain into a chilled martini glass. Garnish with a mint sprig upside down in the glass.

The Queen's garden

2 wheels of cucumber

7 blueberries

10 fresh mint leaves

50 ml gin

15 ml elderflower cordial

75 ml ginger beer

1 sprig of fresh mint, to garnish

1 cucumber wheel and 2 or 3 blueberries, to garnish

1. In a highball glass, muddle the cucumber wheels and the blueberries. Add the mint leaves and top up the glass with crushed ice. Pour in the gin and elderflower cordial and stir it well. Add the ginger beer, mix it gently and top up with crushed ice. To finish, garnish with a mint sprig, a cucumber wheel and the blueberries.

Index

3

Ebury Press, an imprint of Ebury Publishing,
20 Vauxhall Bridge Road,
London, SW1V 2SA

Ebury Press is part of the Penguin Random House
group of companies whose addresses can be found at
global.penguinrandomhouse.com

Copyright © Le Bab 2017
Photography © Justin De Souza 2017

Le Bab have asserted their right to be identified as the
authors of this Work in accordance with the Copyright,
Designs and Patents Act 1988

First published by Ebury Press in 2017

www.penguin.co.uk

A CIP catalogue record for this book is available from
the British Library

Design: Eoghan O'Brien

ISBN 9781785036422

Colour origination by Rhapsody, Ltd, London
Printed and bound in India by Replika Press Pvt. Ltd.

Penguin Random House is committed to a sustainable
future for our business, our readers
and our planet. This book is made from
Forest Stewardship Council® certified paper.